"*Rest in the Storm* is much needed oxygen for breathless people everywhere. Instead of being cheered on by the socially acceptable mantra of 'more and more, faster and faster,' Dr. Jones advises us to rediscover the sacred pace of Jesus. Overload and hurry are not prerequisites for service but mortal enemies of the faith. In writing that often reaches prose-poetry, Jones raises an urgent stop sign: *Stop believing that chronic exhaustion is normal, that a listless spirit is inevitable, that burnout is piety*. His goal? Sustainability, service, passion, and joy. Do your future a favor—buy this book and read it often."

—Richard A. Swenson, M.D.
Author of *The Overload Syndrome: Learning to Live within Your Limits*

"A pastor-scholar speaks from his heart to our hearts about God's care and the place of sabbath in our fast-paced and stressful world. Jones issues an invitation for self-care to be exercised by caregivers and provides practical strategies to make that a reality. This is must-reading for pastors and all those who serve in caring ministries."

—Robert W. Pazmiño
Author of *By What Authority Do We Teach*

"Jones' call for clergy to embrace again our role as spiritual care providers—and not as CEOs, administrators, or builders of programs and buildings—is radical for the African American religious community. His detailing of the consequences for our failure to do so must not be ignored if the African American church is to survive as the potent, competent, life-and-death affirming model that the African American community and the world need."

—Martha Simmons
Coexecutive Editor
The African American Pulpit

"Balance of work and rest is the key to faithful and effective ministry. Do we trust God sufficiently to rest our weary souls in the back of the boat while the storm rages around us? Kirk Jones' resounding summons to personal wholeness and wellness is an essential antidote to the workaholic poison of our age."

—Kate Harvey
Executive Director, Ministers' Council
American Baptist Churches USA

"'What do you do to relax?' This question changed Kirk Byron Jones' life. Written by a scholar with a pastor's heart, *Rest in the Storm* speaks about navigating the storms of life and finding peace. In this well-timed book, Jones explores the unavoidable risks of caregiving and the unnecessary costs we bring on ourselves. Through ample illustrations and practical tools to guide the reader, he invites us to 'float the waters of contentment instead of always scaling the mountains of accomplishment.' *Rest in the Storm* is tender, accessible, challenging, and above all, practical. People who find themselves in positions to care for others will find this a useful and inspiring resource for their lives and work."

—Sharon Thornton
Associate Professor of Pastoral Care
Andover Newton Theological School

"Most ministers and caregivers have an ongoing struggle to learn how to care for themselves. Dr. Jones' book draws the reader in to consider how to live at 'a savoring pace' rather than at the fast pace of life that our culture delivers. The prose is engaging, the personal examples provide authenticity, and the connection to stories from the Bible are helpful. Anyone who reads this book will be fed at a deep level that just might lead to a whole new way of living."

—Linda C. Spoolstra
Executive Minister
American Baptist Churches of Massachusetts

"Kirk Jones risks openness about personal struggle and discovery to provide a greatly needed and vitally useful guide to self-care for caregivers. He offers a biblically and theologically grounded guide, one that is richly textured with personal anecdote and others' stories. I highly recommend it."

—Richard P. Olson
Visiting Professor of Pastoral Care
Central Baptist Theological Seminary

KIRK BYRON JONES

Blessings,

Kirk Byron Jones

REST IN THE STORM

Self-Care Strategies for Clergy and Other Caregivers

Judson Press
Valley Forge

REST IN THE STORM

Self-Care Strategies for Clergy and Other Caregivers

Library of Congress Cataloging-in-Publication Data

Jones, Kirk Byron
Rest in the storm : self-care strategies for clergy and other caregivers / Kirk Byron Jones.
p. cm.
Includes bibliographical references.
ISBN 0-8170-1393-8 (pbk. : alk. paper)
1. Clergy-Job stress. I. Title.
BV4398 .J66 2001
253'.2–dc21 00-060372

Printed in the U.S.A.

07 06 05 04 03 02

10 9 8 7 6 5 4 3

To my mother, Ora Mae Jones,
my first caregiver and
To my departed father, Frederick Jesse Jones,
my finest champion.

Also to the physician in Pennsylvania who asked me,
"What do you do to relax?"

"Come to me, all you that are carrying heavy burdens,
and I will give you rest. Take my yoke upon you,
and learn from me; for I am gentle and humble in heart,
and you will find rest for your souls."

—Matthew 11:28-29

Contents

Acknowledgments

At the invitation of my friend Hector Cortez, associate executive director for biblical justice, American Baptist Churches USA, it was my privilege to serve as a Bible study leader in October 1999. The focus of the Public Mission Team gathered was developing a response to the varied manifestations of violence in our world. Because I am a social ethicist as well as a clergyman, I thought, initially, that I would speak of theological interpretations and solutions regarding social conflict, and make references to my own experiences as a public pastor. I suspected that that was what my hosts were expecting. In my preparation, however, I was led to focus on a form of violence we rarely address: the self-violence that committed clergy and caregivers unleash inadvertently on themselves in the process of caring for others. I am indebted to Rev. Cortez and the Public Mission Team for receiving my detour as an inspired one. Indeed, their intense engagement is the communal catalyst of this book.

I was most fortunate to be in a working relationship with Judson Press prior to this book's publication. I knew from our joint efforts with *The African American Pulpit* that *Rest in the Storm* was in caring, capable hands. I extend heartfelt gratitude to everyone at Judson, most especially Kristy Arnesen Pullen, publisher; Rebecca Irwin-Diehl, book editor; Victoria McGoey, managing editor; Linda Peavy, director of marketing; and my comrade in the early refinement of this work, Randy Frame, acquisitions editor. I must also express my appreciation to Olivia Cloud, who copyedited the original manuscript. Thank you all. I hope that this is just the beginning.

Andover Newton Theological School, its students, staff, and faculty, is a fertile and faithful field of theological inquiry. This book was strengthened by my conversations "on the hill." I am particularly grateful for students in my Spring 2000 class, Creating the Public Church, who read and reviewed portions of this manuscript. Special gratitude is extended to the Reverends Adrienne Berry-Burton and Susan Suchocki-Brown for their review of expanded portions of the manuscript in its first forms.

I thank the members of the four congregations I have served as pastor: Ebenezer Baptist Church, Boston; Beacon Light Baptist Church, New Orleans; Calvary Baptist Church, Chester, Pennsylvania; and First Baptist Church, Randolph, Massachusetts. I am indebted to your support and prayers. I am especially grateful to those of you who took the time to ask me how I was doing, and who, sometimes in vain, encouraged me to slow down and take care of myself. This book is the extended ripple effect of your affection for me and my family.

I thank my family. I am married to a marvelous merry-making wife of twenty years. Bunnie prophesied several years ago that my first book would (and should) be about self-care. I revel in her word and person. Jasmine, Jared, Joya, and Jovonna are our awesome offspring. Their company and laughter had more to do with this book than they will ever know.

Introduction

I am captivated by God, excited by the gospel, and devoted to the church. Yet, there looms an ominous shadow. If God, gospel, and church are so wondrous, why is it that many involved in ministry today are feeling fatigued and empty? On one level, the answer may be all too obvious, albeit unsettling, to admit: Genuine caring and commitment necessarily result in periods—sometimes prolonged periods—of emotional stress and strain. Whether one is a member of the clergy, a nurse, a doctor, a teacher, a social service worker, or even an adult child caring for an ill or aging parent at home, feeling drained and depressed from time to time goes with the territory. Such is the real cost of really caring.

There are discomforting—even dangerous—realities that are, indeed, inseparable from serving and sacrificing for others. However, in light of my own thirty years of clergy experience and fifteen years of professorial inquiry and dialogue, I think other questions need to be asked:

- *To what extent do caregivers experience self-inflicted, unnecessary suffering?*
- *How much of the healer's hurting may be attributed, not to unavoidable costs of caring, but rather to unhealthy beliefs and behaviors regarding the essential relationships between personhood, vocation, recreation, and rest?*
- *Are there alternative understandings and strategies that will allow clergy and other caregivers to minister and serve more frequently out of spiritual, psychological, emotional, and physical abundance, not scarcity?*

A standard preflight practice involves airplane attendants communicating all-important emergency procedures to passengers. Among other things, passengers are informed of air masks that will be released in the event of a serious crisis. Persons traveling with children are given an additional directive: "Place the mask on yourself first; then place the mask over the child's face." The reasoning is readily understandable: The well-being of the child is dependent on the well-being of the child's caregiver. The child's life is more gravely at risk if the caring adult in a moment of crisis is gasping for air. Likewise, care of others in our world—whether from the pulpit, in the classroom, in the hospital room, or elsewhere—is more possible and effective as clergy, educators, and healthcare professionals take care of themselves before, during, and after tending to the needs of others.

In this book, I will discuss beliefs and strategies aimed at helping caregivers care for themselves better. I will refer to matters regarding clergy frequently, but not exclusively. While some of the suggestions for combating commitment overload may resonate with other reading you have done on self-care, some recommendations will, I suspect, be novel, such as "Getting to the Back of the Boat" and "Living Life at a Savoring Pace." Yet, I am hoping that such ideas and practices will become refreshing waters of restful calm for you in the midst of the storms that rage around you and the people in your care. Moreover, my prayer is that whatever your particular work of care-giving might be, you will arrive at an unquestioned certainty, which may be expressed in the following credo: *I am no less precious to God than the work I do or the people I serve.*

In Joy,
Kirk Byron Jones
November 2000

CHAPTER ONE

Naming the Pain

The Tyranny of Too Much

Many people who outwardly appear to be happy and successful are, in reality, living with deep, inner pain. This pain is induced by trying to do too much—trying to be all things to all people. By the thousands, persons are overdosing on over-commitment. More than a few of these persons are clergy and teachers serving in churches and other religious institutions across the country, indeed throughout the world. Day in and day out, they minister with apparent vigor and compassion, but just inches beneath the surface of such a ministry lies a churning undercurrent of discontent. Dive into those waters, and you may find yourself caught in an undertow of pent-up fatigue and frustration.

One of the main reasons for pastoral stress and burnout is the vast number of tasks that pastors are asked to perform, and perform well. The pastor is expected to fulfill a variety of responsibilities and to possess knowledge about a vast array of concerns related to the church and to the community at large. Now let me state emphatically that, more often than not, churches are not knowingly or intentionally abusing their pastors. Rather, I believe the proliferation of unrealistic pastoral expectations in our churches is the result of uncritical acceptance of traditional expectations that are augmented by new demands in our changing world. That having been said, the foregoing is explanation but not justification for pastoral oppression.

The following job description is a real-life example of what a well-intentioned church expected from its pastor. Having reviewed many such descriptions, I know that this one is not an isolated example. In too many instances, it is the expected, if not written, norm.

The Pastor Is Expected to Carry Out the Following Duties as Described Herein:

1. Preach and lead worship at least four Sundays per month. This includes the first and last Sundays of each calendar year.
2. Administer Communion to the congregation on the first Sunday of each month.
3. Conduct funeral services for members of the church. The pastor will contact the bereaved family as soon as possible following the death and meet with them prior to the service.
4. Meet regularly with the diaconate and participate in the training of new deacons.
5. Motivate church leaders and develop new leaders.
6. Consult regularly with the diaconate regarding additions or changes related to the ministry staff.
7. Encourage, support, and direct members who have expressed an interest in or calling to ordained ministry.
8. Be present at church activities and functions.
9. Ensure that the church is active in both national and international missions.
10. Provide spiritual emphasis on financial giving.
11. Teach weekly Bible study.
12. Assist in training Sunday school and Vacation Bible School teachers.
13. Assist the revival committee in planning revivals.
14. Ensure that there is an active and vibrant department of Christian education and Sunday school.
15. Develop an aggressive and comprehensive youth ministry.
16. Visit at least two to three sick or shut-in members per month; provide Communion to each long-standing shut-in member at least once a year.
17. Regularly check on families experiencing crisis.

18. Frequently review membership rolls and become familiar with the congregation, paying close attention to members under watch-care and new converts, as well as to prospective members.
19. Review status reports regarding sick or shut-in members provided by the diaconate and ministerial staff.
20. Play an active role in nominating members to positions of leadership.
21. Encourage voter registration and civic participation.
22. Obtain reports from persons receiving church funds to attend conventions.
23. Foster collaborative efforts with sister churches.
24. Supervise seminarians.
25. Oversee church administrative staff.
26. Ensure that there is an adequate and suitable musical component for the morning worship service.
27. Serve as an ex-officio member of all boards, committees, and auxiliaries.
28. Provide congregation with a schedule of office hours; notify diaconate concerning vacation plans at least sixty (60) days in advance.
29. Coordinate long-range planning and implementation.
30. Coordinate planning and creation of the annual church calendar.
31. Work with the budget committee in the formulation of the annual church budget.
32. Prepare agenda and serve as moderator for the church's joint board meetings, quarterly meetings, and annual business meetings.
33. Monitor the financial contributions of church members.
34. Support the work of the trustee board.
35. Direct and delegate requests to the appropriate boards.

Testimonies from the Trenches

Worse than a church's vision of such an unhealthy and unholy model of pastoral ministry is the fact that many ministers willingly and eagerly sign this premature death certificate! In their eagerness to fulfill their calling, these men and women of God naively covenant with the church to become overworked and stressed out. The tragic and understandable result is that most ministers do not, and cannot, live up to this agreement; they die emotionally and physically as a result of it.

Experience the painful testimony of one servant who was breaking under the enormous physical, mental, and spiritual strain often associated with pastoral ministry:

> I am appalled at what is required of me! I am supposed to move from sick bed to administrative meeting, to planning, to supervising, to counseling, to praying, to trouble-shooting, to budgeting, to audio systems, to meditation, to worship preparation, to newsletter, to staff problems, to mission projects, to conflict management, to community leadership, to study, to funerals, to weddings, to preaching. I am supposed to be 'in charge,' but not *too* in charge—administrative executive, sensitive pastor, skillful counselor, public speaker, spiritual guide, politically savvy, and intellectually sophisticated. And I am expected to be superior, or at least first-rate, in all of them. I am not supposed to be depressed, discouraged, cynical, angry, or hurt. I am supposed to be upbeat, positive, strong, willing, and available. Right now, I am not filling any of those expectations very well . . . and I am tired.[1]

When I first read these words, I cried. I knew that my tears were not just out of empathy, but because the words had hit home. Perhaps I was crying as much for myself as I was for the pastor whose testimony I had read. At that time, I already had been a pastor for fourteen years, and I knew from heart-wrenching experience that the lament was true. Though the theoretical expectation is that pastors serve as mediators for God (a task that is daunting enough by itself), the practical expectation in the minds of many Christians, including pastors themselves, is that the pastor will operate as a little God—a Yahweh Jr., so to speak.

Many ministers, including those just beginning and those nearing the conclusion of their careers, lead lives characterized by overload and hurry. Consider the following testimonies—the first from a seminarian and the second from a seasoned pastor.

> I often have visions of long walks on far away beaches, napping in hammocks, resting lazily with no scheduled place to be. However, these thoughts always place me outside of the realm of everyday life. I am the master of imaging myself relaxing in some remote location, but I fear that I am incapable of visualizing a slower pace in everyday life. I am constantly complaining that I am so busy, yet I delight in telling others how much I do.... I am a seminary student, I teach Sunday school, I sing in the choir, I coordinate a ministry for twenty-somethings. I must love God, otherwise I wouldn't do all this. What is becoming more and more apparent to me, however, is that when one does this much, his/her relationship with the Lord can't grow much beyond the external. That is to say, there are so many observable things going on, little else possibly can be happening in the secret places. There just isn't any time. We get so caught up in trying to do things for God that we forget that all that He wants is for us to spend time with Him. What good is service to God if we have lost the Lord in our purpose for serving?
>
> ***
>
> My wife and I have tried to set aside one "date" evening a month, although you know as well as I how difficult that can be. More than once I have been called away just before we were to leave, or to sit down to eat a "special" meal that my wife had cooked because an emergency had arisen in the church or with a church family. I considered turning off the phone for this one evening, but in good conscience I can't.
>
> It seems that in the back of my mind is the thought, "If only we can get through this next week with all of its activities," but next week or next month always seems to be just as packed. The older I get the more I realize that if I don't take care of myself, the greater chance there is of me getting ill.
>
> I can understand why there are so many problems within clergy

families. The pace that we lead can drive loved ones apart. I thank the Lord for leading me to a person who has stuck by my side through many years of training and ministry. She has eaten far too many meals alone because I have been off somewhere else doing the work of the church.

Tracing the Trouble

Author H. Richard Niebuhr may have been the first to write about the superpastor expectation in his book, *The Purpose of the Church and Its Ministry,* published almost fifty years ago. In his work, Niebuhr identified a trend among pastors to shift out of their more traditional role as spiritual care providers to an expanded ministerial role of "pastoral director"—someone who directs the diverse activities of the congregation. This development has reached its head today as many persons perceive pastors as ecclesiastical CEOs. While I do not mean to denigrate the godly callings of managerial and administrative leadership, the uncritical acceptance of executive pastoral functioning is a major factor contributing to the spread of ministerial overload.

There is another factor that contributes to widespread ministerial overload: ministers who are in denial about the severity of pastoral stress and about its awful pain and negative consequences. The denial is understandable, however. It is easy to trivialize the hurt of personal pain when you have been trained to focus on the pain of others and to regard their pain as being more important than your own or that of your own family.

Sometimes, laudable attempts to diminish the severity of stress induced by unrealistic expectations even succumb to the myth of ministerial invincibility. For example, after suggesting two effective strategies for eliminating overload in the pastorate—communicating with church leaders about the problem and having an awareness of one's own strengths and weaknesses—author Jay Kesler proceeds to give in to the problem, albeit unintentionally:

> But given those remedies, we still have to accept that to some extent,

> we're never going to solve expectation overload entirely. We have to realize that impossible expectations are part of the role we've taken on, part of the harsh reality of life. The job is ambiguous; it is unfair at times; it's occasionally impossible to go to bed at night thinking we've done all we should have that day.[2]

Based on personal experience, I certainly can agree with some of Kesler's concessions; however, I object to the seductive and dangerous spirit of his assertion. He seems to encourage the possibility that we can do a better job of meeting the unrealistic demands placed on clergy if we simply submit to the inevitability of it all. This theory is seductive because it suggests that, with a little acquiescence, we can do the work of superhumans—that we still can be, if not all things to all people, then most things to most people. Moreover, the author encourages a dangerous alliance with overload. Such complicity, practiced by persons who set no boundaries in an environment where there is no limit on expectations, creates chronic fatigue and depression.

We are at a point when too many ministers and their families are suffering needlessly, and the tragic ripple effect is adversely affecting the health of our churches and communities. This suffering is well known, if largely undocumented, in our churches. There are far too many instances of domestic abuse (emotional, verbal, and physical), adultery, parent-child emotional angst, and division among clergy families. Indeed, there are increasing instances of clergy and spousal suicide.

I do not want to suggest that pastors and their families are, or can be, immune to the same realities that wreak havoc on families everywhere. We must, however, come to see the connection between familial breakdown and personal overload more clearly. The result is lives that take on too much and do not allow sufficient time for self-care or for attention to family. Certainly, neglecting personal needs and ignoring self-care are not solely responsible for the escalation of violence, tension, and separation among clergy families; however, self-neglect is an important, if understated, contributing factor.

Clergy members must learn to confess personal overload and hurry as threats to our bodies (self and family), to the body of Christ, and to the body politic. We must confess insufficient self-care as a subtle but lethal expression of personal and social violence.

This leads me to the articulation of an important truth that serves as a fundamental thread running throughout this manuscript: *Well-doing, devoid of proper self-care is, at best, doing well poorly. Exemplary care for others is rooted in vigilant self-care.* A phrase from a prayer written by that most amazing spirit-person, Howard Thurman, former dean of chapel at Howard University and Boston University, serves as the central yearning of this text:

> [God,] Teach us how to respond to the needs of Thy children in ways that do not undermine the self, but inspire and enliven the spirit.[3]

---

[1] Chandler W. Gilbert, "On Living the Leaving," in Edward A. White, ed., *Saying Goodbye* (Bethesda, Md.: The Alban Institute, 1990), 25.

[2] Jay Kesler, *Being Holy, Being Human* (Waco, Tex.: Word Books, 1988), 75.

[3] Howard Thurman, *The Centering Moment* (Richmond, Ind.: Friends United Press, 1969), 115.

CHAPTER TWO

Confessing and Confronting Self-Violence

My Testimony

My own frightening awakening to the reality of self-violence came twelve years ago while I was living in Chester, Pennsylvania. At the time I was a husband, the father of two young children, pastor of Calvary Baptist Church in Chester, and a Ph.D. candidate at Drew University in Madison, New Jersey. In addition, I had said "yes" to more than a reasonable number of community leadership assignments and preaching invitations. At that time, I was living my life in the only way I had ever known. As a young preacher, active student, and church member, I had always done many tasks simultaneously, simply because I could. Persons seemed to benefit from my work, and multitasking fed my joy, as well as my ambition and drive. When I became tired, I rested—but only when I had to, and not for very long. Reflecting on those times, I am glad I can say that my "doing-itus" did not lead to familial neglect, as it often does. Whenever individuals offered unsolicited condolences to my wife over her misfortune of being "married to a minister," she witnessed that she was married to a caring and present husband and father.

Yet the reality was that, through years of meaningful wear and tear and toll-taking ministry service, someone very important to me was going dry from the inside out. Someone was being ignored and neglected. That someone was me. Not the husband-father-preacher-pastor-student me, but the me who was apart from the roles I was fulfilling, the gifts I was manifesting, and the assignments I was tackling. The me who was the child of God, the person whom God loved unconditionally, apart from the trappings of earthly achievement and accomplishment. The me who needed rest and play to temper the activism and labor. The me who needed to float occasionally in the waters of contentment instead of always scaling mountains of accomplishment. The me who measured life not just in terms of his productivity, but in terms of *who* he was and *whose* he was. The me who needed more empty spaces to be still and silent. This me was on the critical list.

That me who had been ignored and suppressed for so long suddenly cried, "No more!" while I was preaching in West Chester one night. Midway through the sermon, I turned to my seminary friend, Earl Trent, then pastor of St. Paul's Church, and said tersely, "I can't go on!" I had come to my limit. I felt no physical pain, just a deep sense of fatigue that told me I could not go on. I had experienced the feeling before, but never to the extent that I needed to end a sermon in progress, and certainly never to the point of being forced to bow to that weariness so abruptly and so publicly.

Physical disturbances arrived soon after that incident. I began having difficulty sleeping. I felt stinging sensations in my arms and legs. Without provocation, at times my heart would begin beating very fast. But most frightening of all, I experienced moments of intense anxiety, as if my every breath would be my last. For a month or more, I was enmeshed in something I had never experienced before—something from which I could not shake loose.

Admittedly, I was more than a little relieved when a physician concluded that my heart was fine and that I was in good physical condition. However, I didn't feel like a person who was in good physical health. I perceived that something inside was still wrong, something mysterious and terrible. As I remember, that "something" was just waiting to be unmasked so that it could explode, exposing the capable exterior I had projected for so long.

My awakening and healing was triggered by a doctor's simple and well-timed question: "What do you do to relax?" Those six words changed my life. At the time he asked, I did not have a ready answer to the question. I think I said something like "I read." But what I did not say was that my reading material was, more often than not, ministry or school related. The doctor began talking softly, in an almost matter-of-fact, off-the-cuff manner about the need for relaxation and rest. My physician cautioned me that I needed to find time to do things outside the realm of my work to relieve stress—the ever-present emotional, physical, and psychological drain on the body. Prior to this consultation with my physician, I do not recall ever having heard the word *stress* before.

Following that eye-opening session with my doctor, I set off in search of the meaning and power of stress in everyday living. Through my investigation, I learned that even when we are doing things that are utterly enjoyable, we expend physical energy. The unavoidable expenditure of human energy, combined with the conscious and nascent light-hearted to heart-wrenching emotional wrestlings of life, creates living friction or stress inside us. Ideally, this internal friction is controlled and channeled productively through exercise, rest, and recreational hobbies. Important events, both negative and positive, understandably create higher levels of stress inside us; friction that usually subsides once the moment of change, crisis, or transition has subsided.

Not only is stress an unavoidable element of life; in many instances it is extremely positive, inducing strength and creativity powerful enough to help us meet the most formidable of challenges. For example, if I suddenly realize that one of my four children is in imminent danger, my stress level will skyrocket. Yet the dramatic increase in my body's response mechanisms actually may enhance my ability to react with appropriate haste and wisdom to prevent harm from coming to my child. Modulated, focused stress is what saves lives in many instances.

But there is an ominous shadow that hovers over stress, brought on not by stress itself, but by the poor management of stress. Stress is an inescapable constant of life. But the consequences of stress greatly depend on the way in which this constant life tension is managed. Momentary, intense stress can preserve life, while chronic, undiluted stress can kill. That night in the West Chester pulpit, my stress level had reached an intensity that demanded immediate withdrawal from the sermonic task at hand. It continued to manifest itself through subsequent physical symptoms of pain, disorientation, and fear.

Ironically, that night of shutdown, along with those subsequent days of burnout, may have saved my life. Since then, I have sought to explore and appropriately live out the necessary (if at times elusive and precarious) balance between self-care and care for others.

The Violence We Do Not Talk About

Some years ago, the late Thomas Merton identified a form of violence to which persons committed to social justice were especially susceptible:

> There is a pervasive form of contemporary violence...[and that is] activism and overwork. The rush and pressure of modern life are a form, perhaps the most common form, of its innate violence.
>
> To allow oneself to be carried away by a multitude of conflicting concerns, to surrender to too many demands, to commit oneself to too many projects, to want to help everyone in everything, is to succumb to violence.
>
> The frenzy of our activism neutralizes our work for peace. It destroys our inner capacity for peace. It destroys the fullness of our own work, because it kills the root of inner wisdom, which makes work fruitful.[1]

If Merton were alive today, he would apply his diagnosis to activists and a great many others who afflict themselves, and others, with the violence of overload and hurry. Such persons may be found in every rank and walk of life.

Notably, Merton identified self-neglect as a form of violence. I do not think it is too strong a word. There is confirmed medical evidence that the consequence of chronic self-neglect—namely, stress—weakens the immune system, thereby making us more vulnerable to colds and diseases, and possibly even to some types of cancer. Stress can cause sleep problems, leaving us fatigued and vulnerable to accidents as well as illness.

In September 2000, a child in Boston died after she spent an entire workday in the back of a steamy car where she had been mistakenly left by her father. He was supposed to drop her off at a day-care center. He realized his tragic error only after driving to the day-care center to pick up his child. Driving to and from work, he was not aware of the child's presence. Given the bases we try to cover and the speed at which we go about covering them, it makes morbid sense that such an accident can happen. Similar incidents have been reported across the country. For these reasons and more, hurry and overload may rightfully be labeled forms of violence. This form of self-violence is particularly potent and prevalent for two primary reasons: social acceptance and easy camouflage.

First, the violence of overload and hurry (at points I will discuss them as one entity because of their close connection) is a socially acceptable form of brutality. Although there is a general consensus of belief that frowns on domestic abuse, substance abuse, and other forms of abuse frequently highlighted in the media, such is not the case with overload and hurry. More often than not, the self-violent perpetrator is rewarded with occupational perks and promotions for repeatedly going above and beyond the call of duty. Indeed, there is the notion that great familial and personal sacrifices are prerequisites to establishing and sustaining a successful career—or, more fundamentally, to assuring economic survival.

As a result, occupational incentives and unchallenged beliefs concerning the significance of work in our lives keep us from identifying the destructive nature of overload and hurry. Pathetically, if understandably, at the funerals of persons who overdid it, we wax on eloquently about how much they gave of themselves, refusing to acknowledge publicly or privately that their superactive lifestyle may have been the very reason for the lauded one's early demise. Our silent consent, in the name of paying homage to the dearly departed, maintains our deathly denial of the high costs of overload and hurry. The detriments of overload and hurry are disguised as exemplary commitment—and this is the second reason hurry and overload are so dangerous. They are constantly and casually rendered indistinguishable from hard work and productive efficiency. We camouflage unhealthy living habits in the rhetoric of unselfish (sacrificial) living.

The self-violence that results from overload and hurry is particularly lethal because of its social acceptability. Moreover, our ability to outfit this self-destruction in garb that disguises its true nature makes it even more menacing. Social acceptance and easy camouflage are the reasons there is no better inducement to overcommitment than religious devotion.

In his book, *Margin: Restoring Emotional, Physical, Financial, and Time Reserves to Overloaded Lives*, Richard Swenson includes the following passage about overload in the Christian church:

> "Christians will run you into the ground," someone once commented. Seeing the great number of needs, pastors and laypeople often place unbearable demands upon themselves—and others. "I think churches may tear a family apart by overloading and overburdening," observes one family ministry pastor.[2]

Great causes, including religious vision and devotion, may inspire great energy, passion, and activism. However, the problem arises when such zeal leads to chronic overload and hurry—when fervor runs roughshod over the no less sacred calling of personal well being. Barbara Brown Taylor is right to assert, "Faithfulness to God is something different from multiple committee memberships and evening meetings."[3]

The Dangerous Cheers from Without

Merton's powerful critique cites "the rush and pressure of modern life" as the "most common influence" of self-violence. Of this fact, there can be no doubt. There are forces in our modern way of life that constantly urge us on like cheerleaders at a football game. The cheer is simple, but dangerous: "More! More! Faster! Faster!"

Many writers have challenged us to reflect on the way our cultural values and expectations have been altered as a result of massive and relatively recent technological advancements. Swenson records no less than twenty-three forms of culturally induced overload, including activity, expectation, fatigue, and hurry. From his reflections on hurry, Swenson writes:

> Haste is a modern ailment. It also is fashionably American. Our lives are nonstop, lived at a breathless pace. We walk fast, talk fast, eat fast, and then excuse ourselves by saying, "I must run." Time urgency is a national emblem. "Hastiness and superficiality—these are the psychic diseases of the twentieth century," accuses Aleksandr Solzhenitsyn. But, as the Finnish proverb teaches, God did not create hurry.[4]

James Ballard has identified what may be the most profound, and personally unsettling, form of cultural change:

> Constant and sudden change allows for less and less time to be spent doing anything resembling a normal state of calm and stability: As we move further into this millennium, the interlocking of change will occur at an even faster rate until finally it becomes a constant, resembling waves in the rapids of a river. We are living in a condition that writer Peter Vaille calls *constant white water*.[5]

The net effect, according to James Gleick, is that we have all become people of speed and restlessness, otherwise known as Type A personalities. In his book *Faster*, Gleick asserts, "Type A is who we are—not just the coronary-prone among us, but all of us, as a society and as an age."[6]

One doctor, lamenting how the priority on speed was undercutting her ability to relate sensitively with patients, commented:

> With the constraints of fifteen-minute visits and productivity quotas, I can't remember the last time I asked a patient, "How are you, really?" and meant it. I don't have time to get beyond the next mammogram, Pap smear, cholesterol or viral load results. [7]

With regard to Christian ministry specifically, I think it is important to point out a prevailing external inducement to hurry and overload. Operative is what I would term an unbalanced theology of sacrifice. There are many Scripture references, not to mention postbiblical examples that tout personal abandonment as a necessary and continuous act of faithful service. Self-sacrifice is a hallmark of our faith, yet in most of the world's great religions, self-care is an equally essential component of spiritual well being. In Christianity, however, the latter is the unsung hallmark, muted and ignored to the detriment of clergy and their families. As a result, the people we have been called to serve we ultimately dis-serve. Unlimited availability feeds a pathological dependency on clergy that is neither healthy, nor spiritual.

The Dangerous Cheers from Within

As we expand our understanding and knowledge about formidable, external cultural contributions to overload and hurry, we must come to terms with certain internal factors as well. The forces from within are far more powerful than external influences because internal forces have the power to multiply the negative effects of the external demands. That is to say, cultural influences may be further enflamed by unhealthy internal realities. But internal forces are also more powerful from a positive aspect. Just as they can enflame negative cultural influences, these forces can, when properly aimed, actually douse the flames of cultural inducements to overload and hurry. In other words, no matter how overwhelming the cultural prompts and cues toward overload, defiant internal resistance can prevail.

In an editorial confession, Kevin A. Miller, editor of the ministerial quarterly journal *Leadership*, identifies three internal areas where overdoing eventually becomes our undoing: achievement, adrenaline, and affirmation from others. (I call them the Three A's.) "It's beautiful to work hard and accomplish much," writes Miller, "but a drive for achievement can wring the water out of a soul, leaving nothing for prayer, joy, patience, family." Beyond recognizing a crippling ambition to achieve, Miller suggests, true confrontation of an overload problem also has to include coming to terms with our addiction to adrenaline—the energy that surges through our system and gives us the "rush" that makes us feel good, at least temporarily. We have to begin to understand that too much of this energy, even when much of it is focused on positive goals, still "wears and tears the body." Miller writes, "To leave a life of chronic overcommitment, we must go through physical withdrawal from adrenaline and learn to live on less of it." Finally, Miller contends that much of our overdoing, "at its root, comes from a need for others to like us."[8]

Noted psychiatrist and author Wayne Oates acknowledged his tendency to overextend himself in this area in his book, *The Struggle to Be Free:*

> I have also concluded that the driving force of my over commitment has been to be accepted, to prove myself worthy, to be a welcome part of the community of those whose approval I considered most worth while....I needed affirmation and overcompensated to get it.[9]

In one episode of the old television series *Little House on the Prairie,* a local pastor lost his church to a charismatic faith healer. Before the new minister was able to assume his responsibilities, however, he was revealed as a fraud. The former pastor was asked to return to his church. On the Sunday of his return, he made a confession. He said that he had been hurt when the church he had served for so long had looked past him in favor of someone else. Additionally, he confessed his envy of the other man's ability to move persons with his great charisma and talent. The old pastor admitted that as he had contemplated his return to the pulpit, he had considered trying to imitate the charismatic figure to which his congregation had been so quickly and passionately drawn. But then he had realized that he only could be himself. It was one question, he revealed, that had brought him peace of mind and heart: *"Is it the duty of a minister to be wanted and loved, or is it the duty of a minister to love the Lord?"*

The Three A's are, of course, blameless in and of themselves. Indeed, achievement, adrenaline, and the desire for affirmation are necessary building blocks of life and civilization. I once heard Rev. Dr. Gardner Taylor ask in one of his sermonic orations, "Where would we be if no one wanted to do anything?" The problem is not the Three A's themselves but, as in the case of Oates, our addiction to those Three A's.

It's Me, O Lord, Standing in the Need of Prayer

I have come to understand that there are formidable obstructions to confessing self-violence, especially in ministry. I characterize them as (1) a lack of personal accountability; (2) a spirit of ecclesial competition; and (3) the denial of personhood.

A Lack of Personal Accountability

We pastor-preachers tend to resist identifying and exposing the weak places lurking inside of us. For some of us, admitting to being vulnerable to the personal affliction of self-violence undermines our image of the minister as a mighty bulwark.

Remember the lyrics of the black church hymn, "It's not my sister or my brother, but it's me, O Lord, standing in the need of prayer"? Truthfully, when it comes to matters of overload and hurry, most of us, if not all of us, are in need of prayer. Acknowledgment of personal responsibility does not just lend the humility and integrity needed in order to assess others' shortcomings; it is the prerequisite step to the spiritual and emotional healing process. As long as we are cut off from our personal maladies, whether through benign ignorance or conscious denial, we ensure that healing never takes place.

Personal accountability plays a critical role in the healing process. It is highly probable that, unless an individual acknowledges that the need exists (whatever it may be) and that it is problematic, the need will go unmet. Other people may not perceive our need. Some may see it but choose not to engage us. Still others may see and confront, but be rebuffed by our resistance to the suggestion that we have a need at all. Self-acknowledgment is integral.

A Spirit of Ecclesial Competition

Another impediment to acknowledging our own self-violence is ecclesial competition. We want to keep this reality quiet, hidden, of course. But most of us want our ministries to manifest the growth and vibrancy of those churches highlighted in our denominational publications. Attention to self-care may be perceived as a weakness, an impediment to achieving "big-church" success.

The mighty minister and successful ministry ideals may form a particularly powerful deterrent to confessing self-violence if the minister is a woman or a member of an ethnic minority. Many women pastors, particularly those who are the first woman to serve in their ministry setting, acknowledge their need to set extraordinarily high standards for service. Women clergy speak of the expectation that they must excel in every function of ministry in order to counter continuing suspicions regarding the legitimacy of their pastoral calling. What an unholy and unjust bind. Fixation on both the real and illusory demands of this ministerial challenge can blind us to the necessary boundaries of recreation and respite in ministry.

The same challenge faces both male and female clergy who are members of ethnic minorities in the United States. Such persons may attempt to meet unrealistic expectations so they will not appear to reinforce a negative racial stereotype. Thus, persons of color may run themselves into the ground in an effort to be twice as effective as members of the dominant racial group. In far too many cases, only through such superhuman efforts have persons of color quelled racist accusations of inferiority and deficiency. Trying to live up to demands that are rooted in racist or sexist beliefs can be deadly.

John Cardinal O'Connor included the following words in his eulogy of Emerson J. Moore, the first black bishop in the Roman Catholic Archdiocese of New York, who died at the age of fifty-seven:

> It is not enough that a black bishop be ordinarily intelligent, he is expected to be extraordinarily intelligent. It is not enough for him to preach adequately, he must preach brilliantly. It is not enough for him to be polite, he must be the essence of courtesy.... In short, if he cannot walk on water, he's an utter failure; if he walks on water too easily, he has forgotten his place.[10]

Women and racial minorities in ministry, as well as in many other caring professions, are often lulled into undervaluing self-care in their pursuit of alien, and ultimately, life-threatening vocational models and expectations. It is a pursuit that organizations and institutions fan, whether wittingly or not, with the allurements of status, power, and in some cases, money. However, almost always, the naive and uncritical acceptance of the committed one results in a sickness and death—spiritually and emotionally, if not physically.

The Denial of Personhood

Yet another influence of self-violence is the denial of personhood. This is perhaps the most common, potent, and disastrous inducement to denying the power of self-violence. In order to genuinely own up to the effects of personal neglect, we must first own up to our reality as persons. The tragic and pervasive problem of ministry is that, along the pathway of service to others, many well-meaning ministerial aspirants forget who they are apart from any religious activity. Their personhood, disconnected from collar and calling, is swallowed up. They become holy dead persons walking.

Dr. Wayne W. Dyer's words about role usurpation are deeply and undeniably true:

> The more your position becomes defined as who you are, the more difficult it is for you to know truth and freedom. The role identification itself can keep you away from your own true higher self, since the role of occupation is the dominant force in your life.[11]

Overvaluing your role versus your personhood is easy to do when your job requires so much of your being, so much of you. Martha Nilsen, one of my former seminary students, made this connection for me:

> Ministers who enjoy their work do so, in part, because their jobs encompass all their being. That being is the same both "on the job" as "off the job," which makes defining when one is off the job more difficult.

Martha's point is an important one. However, it should not be used to justify continued self-violence in our vocation. Although the task of role-person distinction may be difficult, it is infinitely more achievable as we develop a finer, stronger sense of ourselves as persons, separate and distinct from anything we do, including ministry.

It is easy to dismiss the reality of self-violence when there is no perceived self to whom violence can be done. Denying self-violence is evidence of the deepest wound that it may inflict: the refutation of self. For such persons, owning up to self-violence is no less than a defiant, redemptive cry of new life. Not only is the reality of new life at stake, but the possibility of authentic ministry is threatened as well. No long treatise is needed here; rather, the truth is concisely implied in a question raised by Fred Lehman, a former student of mine: *"How can we accept and love the humanity in those we serve if we don't accept and love the humanity of ourselves?"*

As ministers and caregivers, we need to face our self-violence. We must name it and own up to it if we are to be healed. And because self-violence is a lifestyle for many of us, confessing and overcoming a long-standing practice of self-brutality is an extended process. We will need to name and face our unhealthy and unholy addictions continuously, until we are fully delivered. Even then, complete deliverance will require unceasing vigilance.

---

[1] As quoted in Wayne Muller, *Sabbath* (New York: Bantam Books, 1999), 3.

[2] Richard Swenson, *Margin* (Colorado Springs: NavPress, 1992), 85.

[3] Barbara Brown Taylor, "Divine Subtraction," *The Christian Century*, November 3, 1999, 1057.

[4] Swenson, 84-85.

[5] James Ballard, *What's the Rush?* (New York: Broadway Books, 1999), 35.

[6] James Gleick, *Faster* (New York: Pantheon Books, 1999), 20.

[7] Dr. Sondra S. Crosby quoted in "Critical Condition," Mac Daniel, *Boston Sunday Globe*, March 26, 2000, 1.

[8] Kevin A. Miller, "Editorial," *Leadership*, Winter, 1997, 3.

[9] Wayne Oates, *The Struggle to Be Free* (Philadelphia: The Westminster Press), 133.

[10] John Cardinal O'Connor as quoted in "Death of a Bishop: Of Holy Orders and Human Frailty," Joe Sexton, *The New York Times*, October 7, 1995, 21-22.

[11] Wayne W. Dyer, *Your Sacred Self* (New York: HarperCollins, 1995), 46.

CHAPTER THREE

The Back of the Boat

Calming the Storm Inside

During my bout with stress in Chester, Pennsylvania, life took a dramatic turn for the better one night while I was reading Scripture. My wife and children had gone visiting for a few hours and I was alone in the house. Filled with feelings of fear and frustration, I sat down to find some inner strength from the book I had used so often to inspire others. My fingers passed through several passages, but the one that spoke most urgently to me that night was Mark 4:35-41:

> On that day, when evening had come, he said to them, "Let us go across to the other side." And leaving the crowd behind, they took him with them in the boat, just as he was. Other boats were with him. A great windstorm arose, and the waves beat into the boat, so that the boat was already being swamped. But he was in the stern asleep on the cushion; and they woke him up and said to him, "Teacher do you not care that we are perishing?" He woke up and rebuked the wind, and said to the sea, "Peace, be still!" Then the wind ceased, and there was a dead calm.

This Scripture touched me deeply. Suddenly, in my mind, I was the one on a boat in a raging storm. For the past few weeks I had been caught in the storm of my life. Never before had I felt so vulnerable, and so unable to control what was going on in my own mind and body. As the tears began to roll down my face, I prayed, "Lord, I'm in my storm now. I need you to calm my storm." In the next moments I began to feel like I was enveloped by a peaceful calm. A sense of ease washed over me. Suddenly, I was not so afraid anymore. I felt relief and new energy welling up inside me.

Mark's passage was a gift of healing to me that night. Through the years, I continued to refer to it for personal strength, as well as to offer others encouragement when facing stressful conditions. Over the years, I have come to understand Mark's passage as not only a literary source of relief, but also as a living model for learning how to cope with conditions of overload and overdrive. Jesus' actions on the boat that night can guide us out of our storms of stress, and can keep us from needlessly riding into such storms in the first place. I am convinced that both what happened and what did *not* happen on the boat that night offer critical insights into resisting overload and overdrive in everyday living. If we can understand and practice the behaviors Jesus exhibited on the boat, we can experience peace amid the storms of life-threatening stress.

Jesus and the Back of the Boat

Although I had read Mark's account of Jesus calming the sea many times, that particular day, I gained new insight into how Jesus might have handled the demands that were being placed on him. All day long, Jesus had been teaching from the bow of a borrowed boat. For the hundreds who gathered to hear the Teacher that day, the serene waters served as a splendid backdrop to his scintillating stories about lamps, bushel baskets, and mustard seeds. He used the ordinary around them to explode the extraordinary inside them. As dusk approached, Jesus brought his teaching session to a close. His disciples gathered around him, and the portable pulpit became a ferry to the next stop on their truth-telling journey.

As they made themselves comfortable for the roughly ten-mile trek to shore, one by one the disciples realized that, not only had Jesus taken leave of the crowd, he was taking leave of them, too! I can imagine that about that time, Peter approached Jesus with a story that he just knew Jesus was going to love. Before Peter could begin the story, though, Jesus politely waved him off. Judas, the group's treasurer, had been waiting for some time to present Jesus with a plan for securing additional revenue for their rapidly expanding ministry. The Savior walked past him and said, "Let's talk about it later." Just then, James and John queried Jesus about the coming kingdom and their new status and seating in it. Jesus responded to them with a glare. (Perhaps it was like the look senior saints gave us as children when we were out of line in church. There was no mistaking what one look from one of them meant!)

Jesus walked past James and John and made his way to the lower deck. He entered a back room and shut the door behind him. He opened the door again, but just long enough to place a sign outside that read, "Do Not Disturb."

The Synoptic Gospels (Matthew, Mark, and Luke) tell us that Jesus fell asleep while he was in the back of the boat. *Three cheers for the sleeping Savior!* Of all the artistic depictions of Jesus I have seen, I do not believe I have ever seen a picture of Jesus asleep. Perhaps our perceptions of the ever-busy, ever-ready Jesus feed our own addiction to busyness. But, as Mark's account in his Gospel indicates, Jesus was not always busy; more to the point, Jesus slept. *Extra! Extra! Read all about it! The Savior actually slept!* Jesus' perfection did not exempt him from taking care of the human body that he occupied. Jesus ate, became weary, slept, and experienced a broad range of human emotions as well. Sleeplessness is a primary symptom of a person who is over-committed. The consequences are costly in more ways than one:

> American society is sleep-deprived, and the problem is growing. People mistakenly think sleep is a waste of time. They don't realize they'll be more productive if they get more sleep.
>
> Fatigue is to blame for 60% to 90% of all industrial accidents and more than 100,000 highway crashes a year. Sleepy workers cost American companies $18 billion a year in lost productivity.[1]

On the ministerial front, more than a few accidents of judgment and crashes of morality have occurred, in part due to physical and emotional fatigue. If Jesus had simply fallen asleep in the back of the boat, his actions would have been enough of an example for us. But I believe it is likely that he did more than that. When I go to bed, rarely do I just fall asleep. Sometimes I read; other times I reflect on the events of the day. At times I watch television or listen to music. Often I talk with my wife or enjoy playful moments with her before retiring. Perhaps Jesus carved a bit before he went to sleep. Remember, he was a carpenter before he was a preacher. Maybe Jesus looked out the portal of the vessel and allowed himself to be mesmerized by the waves below and the stars above.

We cannot be certain of all that Jesus did while he was in the back of the boat, but we know there were some things that he did not do. Since he was the only one back there, we know that he did not preach to anyone, he did not teach anyone, and he did not heal anyone. While Jesus was in the back of the boat, he was not engaged in ministry to others.

We must learn to make it to the back of the boat if we are to overcome self-violence in ministry. "The back of the boat" is a metaphor, a symbol of the necessary break from the activism of life, in general, and the rigors of ministry, in particular. The back of the boat is not a luxury. Time spent in the back of the boat is not optional if our intention is to lead a healthy, balanced, and productive life. It is the back-of-the-boat time—the "off" time—that makes the bow-of-the-boat time—the "on" time—possible.

Richard Swenson would say that when Jesus went to the back of the boat, he was practicing *margin:*

> [Margin] is the space that once existed between our load and our limits. Margin is the space between vitality and exhaustion. It is our breathing room, our reserves, our leeway. It is the opposite of overload....[2]

When Jesus went to the back of the boat that evening, it was neither the first nor the last time he practiced margin. There are several texts that reveal Jesus at prayer, usually early in the morning. Moreover, there are texts wherein Jesus appeared to be practicing margin as the winds of ministry were blowing. One such time was when Jesus stooped to the ground and began writing while a mob demanded capital punishment for the woman caught in adultery. Often, that moment is interpreted as Jesus providing time for the mob to judge themselves. Why can it not be seen, as well, as a moment when Jesus centered and steadied himself for that challenge and the procession of challenges to come?

Blockades to the Back of the Boat

Earlier, I envisioned some of the disciples standing between Jesus and the rear of the ship. In ministry, we face formidable obstructions to getting to the back of the boat. Here, I am referring to more than the intermittent surprises that arise at the precise moment we wished to have to ourselves; for example, your child's basketball or soccer game that you had promised to attend. These surprises always will arise, but they are not the real obstructions to the back of the boat. The real barriers are two great delusions, and one great denial.

Indispensability

The first delusion is the myth of our own indispensability. In order for us to embrace the time we need and deserve to rest and refuel, we must believe the unbelievable, the preposterous, and the absurd—namely, that life will go along just fine during our temporary retreat. Indeed, things may go even better without us. Often, it is when we move out of the picture that we allow for the necessary leadership shifts and decision-making to take place in our various ministry settings. Believing ourselves to be an essential, indispensable element of a program or institution is a terrible liability, and an outright lie! The layered liability is egoism and overload as we try to live up to the demands of inflated importance. The lie, and an idolatrous one at that, is to bow down to the god of personal irreplaceability. Although none of us are replaceable as unique persons, each of us *is* replaceable with regard to our job or vocation—many of us more so than we ever could stand to admit.

To get to the back of the boat with greater frequency and faithfulness, we must confess our belief in the myth of personal indispensability, and then shake loose of it. Shaking it is no easy task, however, especially if our self-worth is tied exclusively to the ministerial garment. Moreover, in the history of Christian ministry, there is this thread of ecclesiastic indispensability, proudly affirmed in the following quotation attributed to the great Charles Haddon Spurgeon:

> A minister, wherever he [or she] is, is a minister, and should recollect that he [or she] is on duty; a policeman or a soldier may be off duty, but a minister never is.[3]

The fact is that many congregants and clergy alike behave as though ministers are never off duty. For example, friendly conversations at a social gathering or a supermarket can turn into mini-counseling sessions if clergy are not careful. Neither the minister nor the person (or group of persons) talking with the minister intends for it to happen; it just happens. Notably, it is often the minister who will initiate such conversations by asking how a person is doing concerning a matter previously discussed. This is not the only way that a minister's "off" time can easily slip into "on" time. Another way is when ministers are drawn into ministry-related conversations with one another while engaged in activity designed for recreation. Perhaps the most prevalent form of hidden ministry is thinking about ministry-related issues during vacations and other "off" times.

The fact is that ministers, with others and among ourselves, initiate many of these hidden moments of ministry. The moments are hidden because, while such encounters often involve intense listening and sharing, rarely are they acknowledged as moments of ministry that withdraw from the minister's deposits of energy—energy that needs to be replenished.

I do not mean to discount the value of hidden or "soft" ministry; unplanned informal conversations can be both meaningful and helpful. The problem is being unaware that we are working when we think we are at rest. The problem is not taking soft ministry into consideration when we plan our schedules, ensuring that we have ample time to cover the unsuspected energy drains that occur in casual conversations. Better planning can help us to limit soft ministry when we are at rest and to learn how to do soft ministry and all ministry so that we receive even as we are giving.

While the foregoing offers explanation for Spurgeon's vision of the divine eternal on-ness of ministers, I do not think it is justification. With all due respect to a great servant of God and the spirit of commitment Spurgeon sought to evoke, to practice his pronouncement fully is never to get to the back of the boat. To accept Spurgeon's definition of commitment is to accept uncritically the myth of human indispensability. Moreover, unnoticed and unabated soft ministry, combined with intentional ministry, can slowly drain us of the joy of our vocation. The added hurt is that we become joyless, without ever realizing when or why it happened.

In some instances, ministerial indispensability is the offspring of longstanding cultural and political realities, as in the case of ministers in the African American church. It is important for black pastors to know that as they attempt to make it to the back of the boat with greater frequency, they are walking in the face of awesome historical winds. In his seminal work, *The Black Preacher in America,* Charles V. Hamilton linked the extraordinary religious and social expectations surrounding black preachers to the central role of the church in the black community prior to the 1930s:

> The church was pretty much unrivaled in the black community as the major institution of black folk. There were no labor unions; there were few other social, political, or economic agencies in the black community among the lower class. Thus the church was the center.[4]

The black pastor emerged as the undisputed central figure of this pivotal institution:

> Out of this environment came the natural leadership of the black preacher. His [or her] position propelled him [or her] to the front. He [or she] was always given a seat on the platform. He [or she] was sought after by whites who wanted to reach the black community, either to receive or give information. The black preacher was the natural, most convenient funnel. Blacks knew this and they would, more frequently than not, turn to their ministers to intercede for them with the white establishment.[5]

Notably, many ministers served in this mammoth, multifaceted role while engaged in other employment because their congregations were often too small and poor to provide them with adequate financial compensation.

Although the black church shares leadership in the black community with many organizations, it still is regarded as a pivotal point of communal solidarity and activism. There is the continuing expectation that pastors provide leadership on a number of fronts. But voices of pastoral resistance are emerging. For the first time, black pastors are beginning to confess publicly the shadow side of unrealistic expectations. Responding to a question I asked about advising pastors on avoiding the unnecessary pains of ministry, leading black church cleric Dr. E.V. Hill offered a lengthy and revealing response that sheds light on the depth and deadly nature of ministerial indispensability:

> There are several things that lead into the hazard of ministerial overload and the pain that comes with it. One is trying to be all things to all people. I think maybe we are coming out of a twenty-five-year period in which pastors were called on to do so much in the community. We were forced to. Take me for instance. If there is a crisis in the schools, they get Dr. Hill on the phone, even though Dr. Hill is not a school official. If there is a big political question or a racial uprising, "Where is Dr. Hill?" A black college is closing, "Call Dr. Hill."
>
> And the challenge is that I am expected to have something of importance to say about these issues. Now if I were a dentist and twenty-five persons were waiting to see me, in all probability they all would want to see me about teeth. That's not the case with ministers. If you see twenty-five people, it may be that you will deal with twenty-five different issues.[6]

Dr. Hill also linked demanding communal expectation with damning ministerial indispensability and its various hidden, but no less lethal levels:

> Now we need to be careful. Sometimes the expectation that we meet all these demands convinces us that we can. This can give us a messianic complex that is destructive to the preacher and the preacher's family. This messianic complex can work on us so that we can feel bad about not being able to solve all the problems that

> are brought to us. This is a horrible addiction. There is glamour and glee in thinking that you have the answer to many problems and feeling that others think so. It is very seductive, and we can become addicted to it. And it is subtle; we want to endear people to us, but this can lead to people expecting too much from us, and us expecting too much from ourselves.[7]

Being saved from deeply entrenched, unrealistic ministerial expectations involves radical reformations of ministerial understandings and behaviors on the part of ministers and their congregations.

Shaking indispensability takes the kind of initiative and continuing effort displayed by noted pastor Eugene Peterson and the members of Christ Our King Church in Bel Air, Maryland. The shaking process began after Peterson abruptly resigned his pastorate one night. The immediate catalyst was hearing one of his children tell him the exact number of evenings he had been away from home in recent weeks. Peterson recalled the struggle and the liberation of embracing a new model of ministry:

> [Church leaders] wanted to know what was wrong. "Well," I said, "I'm out all the time, I'm doing all this administrative work, serving on all these committees, and running all these errands. I want to preach, I want to lead the worship, I want to spend time with people in their homes. That's what I came here to do. I want to be your spiritual leader; I don't want to run your church."
>
> They thought for a moment and then said, "Let *us* run the church."
>
> I'll never forget what happened because of that talk. Two weeks later, the stewardship committee met, and I walked into the meeting uninvited. The chairman of the group looked at me and asked, "What's the matter? Don't you trust us?" I admitted, "I guess I don't, but I'll try." It took a year or so to deprogram myself.[8]

Although we ministers tend to blame others for our busyness, Peterson realized, as we all must, that we have the power to curtail a great deal of our own overload by facing up to the monster of indispensability within.

Invincibility

The second delusion that may keep us from making it to the back of the boat is the myth of our invincibility. Deep down within, a great many of us feel that we have limitless reserves of compassion and energy. Like the bunny rabbit in the battery commercial, we feel like we can "keep going and going and going." It is not that we completely ignore the signs of fatigue and exhaustion, but we condition ourselves to rest only as we near the breaking-point—and even then just long enough to feel the first pulsations of renewed energy. The result is a life always on the brink of fatigue—or, even more tragic, an early death resulting from cumulative stress and tension. Although a brief respite may give us energy to meet the next need, a rhythm of near exhaustion, interspersed with interludes of rest, will lead to a chronic exhaustion from which recovery may not be possible.

During the writing of this manuscript, my car was being repaired. I was told that it needed a new starter. So, one day when the car did not start in the grizzly cold weather, I wasn't completely surprised. Some months before, I had tried turning the ignition and nothing had happened. After a few more turns it *had* started, but I had known then that a repair was imminent. Even the best makes of automobiles give out and need repairs from time to time. Even the best of God's servants give out, too—but like my car, our bodies and minds give us some advance warning. As ministers, we should recognize those warning coughs and sputters as reminders that we are not beyond giving out, that we cannot just keep going and going and going.

Contributing to this sense of ministerial invincibility (which I think we act out more unconsciously than consciously) are our culture's Three A's of adrenaline, achievement, and affirmation. Yet ministry has its own set of peculiar contributing factors. For one, we are in a profession that usually places us in the role of helping others with matters of deepest meaning and importance. Not only are we called to minister to others in a deep place, but we are expected to minister in a variety of such deep places, including significant life transitions such as death.

A third factor that may contribute to our sense of invincibility is our perceived proximity to God. It is possible, with no small assistance from some congregants, for we ministers to think of ourselves as "god juniors" as opposed to the limited servants of God that we are. And if we assume the role of superman or superwoman, we soon discover that many persons around us will offer to clean and press our costumes and even assist us in putting them on.

The trappings of ministry may be another temptation toward false notions of invincibility and omnipotence. For example, most of us address the congregation from raised positions. We are, for a moment with the Word, "above it all." But the most innocuous and frequent inducement to invincibility may be the titles afforded clergy in the various religious traditions, titles such as "Most Reverend" and "Right Reverend."

Although it may be wishful thinking to believe that ministers will radically alter our architecture and professional vocabulary, it is imperative that we become more alert to these and other unintentional contributors to ministerial invincibility. Any one of these factors is not enough to breed the pseudo strength we are calling into question, but united, these factors become a torrent of lethal suggestion.

We can understand the combined power of various inducements of ministerial invincibility by referring to Marilyn Frye's analysis of systemic oppression. She simply and wisely points out that the singular bars of a cage are not what keeps a bird from free flight, but the bars aligned with one another:

> If you look very closely at one wire in the cage, you cannot see the other wires. If your conception of what is before you is determined by this myopic focus, you could look at that one wire, up and down the length of it, and be unable to see why a bird would not just fly around the wire anytime it wanted to go somewhere. . . . It is only when you step back, stop looking at the wires one by one, microscopically, and take a macroscopic view of the whole cage, that you can see why the bird doesn't go anywhere; and then you will see it in a moment. It will take no great subtlety of mental powers. It is perfectly *obvious* that the bird is surrounded by

> a network of systematically related barriers, no one of which would be the least hindrance to its flight, but which, by their relations to each other, are as confining as the solid walls of a dungeon.[9]

Similarly, any one factor related to ministerial invincibility is not what damns ministers; it is many factors experienced simultaneously and consecutively that turn ministry into an experience of bondage.

The Great Denial

Earlier in this chapter, I indicated that two formidable delusions and one great denial hinder ministers from making it to the back of the boat. The delusions are overdone notions of indispensability and invincibility. The great denial is subjugating the most precious gift that God offers to each of us—personhood.

My sensitivity to personhood was piqued in a way that it never had been before while reading a biography about the influential and deeply spiritual writer/pastor, Henri Nouwen. Michael Ford's biography about the late priest, entitled *Wounded Prophet,* reveals delicate truths about some of Nouwen's deepest struggles. During one such struggle, Nouwen was blessed to have the healing hands and hearts of close friends at his service. Ford points out the specific place of healing for Nouwen during this time of painful transformation:

> There were huge parts of [Nouwen's] personality that he had never allowed himself to look at or consider, because being successful had been such a driving force in him. He had become a fine priest, a good scholar, a talented linguist, a brilliant teacher, and a popular writer, but all that had been only one highly developed side of his personality. There were other areas that the Gavigans discovered were underdeveloped: his ability to be faithful in friendships, to trust love, to believe his value regardless of his gifts, and to have significant relationships that were not based on what he could do or what he could produce—in other words to be a person. Henri had, for so much of his life, lived through his gifts and, because he had a calling, his gifts facilitated his calling and his calling

> facilitated his gifts. Slowly and painfully Henri came to see a much wider panorama of awareness, possibility, and being—one that he had always been denied or had denied himself.[10]

Though Nouwen's extraordinary gifts are rarely found in a single individual, his highlighted shortcoming may be found in many places, including many pulpits. Many of us are overly driven; many of us live exclusively though our gifts and ministerial offices. Thus, many of us need to be liberated from the tyranny of measuring life only in terms of what we do. *Before you are a minister, a preacher, a teacher, or a pastor, and even before you are a parent, spouse, or friend, you are a child of God, a person whom God loves unconditionally.*

I think that there are two ways we inadvertently abandon our humanity, our personhood. First, we may inadvertently discard legitimate personhood along with the garbage of selfishness and egoism. As we seek to dodge praise from others, we unwittingly may wipe away any sense of ourselves as persons. Such individuals are those among us who seem to have difficulty accepting compliments. They quickly divert praise away from themselves to others, or often to God. Of course, going public with one's sense of dependency on others, especially God, is commendable. The problem is not in acknowledging the place of others in our achievements, but in failing to humbly see and value ourselves.

To not see yourself is to be rendered blind to one of God's greatest works—you. Good theology honors God and God's creation in the same breath. This is not merely holy theology; this is healthy theology.

Second, we throw away our sense of personhood as we reach for achievement after achievement, becoming unable to see ourselves, clearly and appreciatively, apart from what we do and produce. The self is hidden behind masks and costumes of endless doing and striving. In both cases, false humility on the one hand and frenzied scurrying on the other, we are unable to observe and celebrate our pure personhood. Authentic spirituality celebrates divinity and humanity, including personal humanity.

What does all of this have to do with the back of the boat? Jesus made it to the back of the boat easily and regularly because he knew that as much as he was a healer, preacher, and teacher, he was something else—

something more, something deeper. He was a child of God. And as a child of God, he needed time for soul nurturing. He needed time to listen to his heart and to yoke his heart with God's heart afresh and anew. He needed time to receive instead of give, as was his norm. He needed time to delight in what, for the moment, he had no responsibility in doing. He needed time to relish being for being's sake. With a transformed sense of personhood, the back of the boat is perceived as a delightful necessity, not a luxury of the lazy. It is a place where our being is replenished for life and for service. It is a sacred place. It is the prerequisite place that makes traversing the terrain of ministry possible.

In 1784 Sir Henry Raeburn, one of Scotland's most popular painters, painted *The Reverend Robert Walker Skating on Duddingston Loch*. In the picture, a church minister is ice-skating, very properly and rigidly, but ice-skating nonetheless. In addition to his manner, the minister's clothing is indicative of his "reverendness." His conservative black suit, stockings, and hat are a dead give-away. One of the messages I receive from the painting is that, even while engaging in a recreational activity, this man was undoubtedly *The Reverend Robert Walker.*

If we are not careful, we can allow ourselves to be completely overtaken by roles and expectations that, while helping to make us who we are, should never define us completely. As I gazed at the picture, I wondered if there ever were times when the Reverend Robert Walker was simply Robert, or Bob, or even Bobby. Did he have a sense of his own holy and unique personhood apart from the black suit and apart from his role as a minister? Was he capable of celebrating life, not just as a member of the clergy but also as a child and as a child of God?

The case can be made that the picture doesn't represent the minister's perception of himself, but the artist's perception of the minister. This is true. But is it not also true that how others perceive us is highly influenced by how we perceive ourselves? The fact is that many clergy radiate an air of religiosity that, more than anything else about us, we wish to have noticed and respected. People see us as ministers not just *first* but often *only,* because tragically, that is the cue we communicate. I believe this is tragic because the associated signal is that ministers *do not* wish to be seen and valued as parents, as spouses, or as ordinary persons.

The back of the boat is that place where we may go to remember who and whose we are. It is the place where roles and responsibilities are no longer the matters at hand. What matters in the back of the boat is that we receive a refreshing of mind, body, and spirit. What matters in the back of the boat is that we are at peace with ourselves and with our God, regardless of life's circumstances. What matters in the back of the boat is that delight is found, not in what we produce, but in what we can, if only for a moment, open ourselves to receiving unconditionally.

---

[1] Tamar Asedo Sherman, "Nap for Success," *USA Weekend*, June 9-11, 2000, 11.

[2] Richard A. Swenson, *The Overload Syndrome* (Colorado Springs: NavPress, 1998), 15.

[3] Ray Jennings, "Back to the Pastorate," *Input*, February, 1990, 1.

[4] Charles V. Hamilton, *The Black Preacher in America* (New York: William Morrow and Company, 1972), 13.

[5] Ibid., 14.

[6] E. V. Hill in "An Interview with E. V. Hill and H. Beecher Hicks Jr.," Kirk Byron Jones, *The African American Pulpit*, Spring 2000, 126.

[7] Ibid.

[8] Eugene B. Peterson, *Subversive Spirituality* (Grand Rapids, Mich.: Eerdmans, 1995), 217.

[9] Marilyn Frye, "Oppression," *Race, Class, and Gender in the United States*, ed. Paula S. Rothenberg (New York: St. Martin's Press, 1999), 146.

[10] Michael Ford, *Wounded Prophet* (New York: Doubleday, 1999), 166.

CHAPTER FOUR

Getting to the Back of the Boat

Creating Back-of-the-Boat Time

It is one thing to appreciate the value of respite; it is another thing to create more of it in our everyday lives. One thing is for sure—getting the back-of-the-boat time you long for and deserve will never happen if you do not *make* it happen.

As well meaning as family, friends, and church members try to be, they are not responsible for setting aside enough time for your personal replenishment; you are! Realizing this is perhaps the first concrete step toward making respite a daily habit in your life. Subsequent action includes developing attitudes and strategies that will change you and your ministry for the better.

Acceptance

It takes great energy to accept the need to retreat to the back of the boat. We face layered resistance to the notion. Our addictions to adrenaline, achievement, and affirmation are formidable. Our overdone notions of indispensability and invincibility are rigid. The self-subjugation of who we are as persons seems to be almost innate to many of us. But if we are to be saved, the awareness of our need must sink down into the deep places. Our own pain can lead us there.

Fannie Lou Hamer, the late legendary singer/activist from Mississippi, once explained her continuing commitment to demanding and dangerous participation in the civil rights movement this way: "All my life I've been sick and tired. Now, I am sick and tired of being sick and tired." We need to own up to being sick and tired of being overloaded and hurried. The empowerment underlying that acceptance is the source of our liberation from the overload we have been denying.

The Big Small Word

Recognizing and then rejecting our condition is one strategy for getting to the back of the boat. Another method may take some practice, but the positive effects can be immediate. In order to perform this task, you may need to practice in front of a mirror in your home or office. In fact, do it right now. Stand in front of a mirror, moisten your lips, take a deep breath, and say the word "No!"

How did that feel? Try it again. This time, say it a little more forcefully. Keep saying it. See yourself saying it, and hear yourself saying it in various settings. The source of a great deal of our overload and the resulting hurry is our acceptance of too many responsibilities—many more than we could ever expect to do well, if at all. The signs of "yes-itus" are all around us: date-books with no empty spaces, unfinished tasks, yellow reminder notes all over the place. Sometimes we scribble multiple notes on the same matter to ensure that we do not forget the thousand things that need to be done "ASAP" and the thousand things that, apparently, we alone are capable of doing. It is almost as if the eleventh commandment is the one we most dread breaking: "Thou shalt not say 'No.'"

One of the late Gwendolyn Brooks's melodic and profound poems is entitled "Do Not Be Afraid of No." Many ministers live as though we are afraid of the word "no." Our sense of personhood and professionalism seems to demand that all requests be accepted and satisfied. Many of us are held in bondage to distorted definitions of self and service that are fixated on endless doing and giving. Are we any less human and any less servants of Christ when we decline invitations that require our personal involvement? Was Jesus any less God's Son when he went to the back of the boat?

Not accepting every enlistment that is placed before us is one of the simplest, most effective ways to overcome self-violence. If we were at a restaurant and the food kept coming long after our hunger had been satisfied, wouldn't we say "No, thank you"? Our challenge is to remember that just because we are asked to do something, and just because we *can* do something (no matter how laudable the task), that capability does not mean we ought to accommodate that request. We have the right, and sometimes even the obligation, to say "No, thank you."

Moreover, our "no" opens the way to someone else's "yes." We inadvertently sabotage leadership development in our churches when we monopolize service opportunities. Our saying "yes" to everything prevents someone else from learning, growing, and contributing. As we say "no" and get out of the way more often, our churches are strengthened via greater participation from those who were formerly locked out by the "yes" of others.

You will know that you really have arrived *when you are able to decline long before you are forced to, and more importantly, before you reach your breaking point.*

Planning Back-of-the-Boat Time

Do you want to know something? When Jesus went to the back of the boat that day, I do not think it was a spontaneous action on his part. I believe that Jesus planned to take a moment for himself. I think that prior to the start of ministry that day (or somewhere along the way) Jesus made a mental note to himself that at some point during the day he would downshift to get some rest. While some of the best back-of-the-boat times are those moments that happen spontaneously, the planned times, I think, sensitize us more to the spontaneous times. If we do not plan times of rest, we are less likely to notice and appreciate the surprising moments that invite us to stop and relax.

Waiting until events and circumstances allow for rest—or until sickness demands it—results in far too little time being spent at the back of the boat. We need to pray, play, and rest regularly to experience life as more of a blessing than a curse. The only way we may be sure to get regular doses of deep quality communion, delight, and respite is to plan them. Each of us needs to establish and obey our own stop signs.

I have found that the best way to ensure that I have sufficient back-of-the-boat time is to schedule such times with the same purposefulness with which I schedule study sessions, meetings, and speaking engagements. I recommend scheduling such times at the beginning of each month. Planning back-of-the-boat time in advance is a way to prevent hurry and overload from occurring. Moreover, I have found that advanced planning creates a deeper commitment to taking that personal time. If such time is important enough to plan early, it is important enough to observe when the time comes.

Deciding how much time to set aside for personal renewal and when to do it is a matter of individual preference and need. I am committed to spending one day per week and several hours each day in the back of the boat. My back-of-the-boat day (commonly referred to as sabbath) is Friday. My daily back-of-the-boat hours usually occur in the early morning between 5:00 and 7:00 A.M., and again at the end of the day, after my family time. I not only plan to have this time, but I generally plan how I am going to spend that time on a "Back-of-the-Boat Schedule." This is a single sheet that I use for planning, in addition to my daily calendar. The difference between them is that, while there are some recreational events on my regular calendar, there are no work-related items on my Back-of-the-Boat Schedule. This single sheet of paper contains such entries as "Read new play by Dario Fo" or "Listen to Ellington." This sheet, kept in view and just an arm's length away, serves two purposes: (1) it stirs up anticipation in me, and (2) it helps me to review my attendance in the back of the boat.

At the end of the week, I review the sheet to determine whether or not I did what I planned to do. This sheet is my way of ensuring that I get the time I need in the back of the boat. I do not always abide by the sheet, however; I may do something else on the spur of the moment, different from what I had planned. The sheet supplies just one more incentive to take my back-of-the-boat time seriously, in a joyful sort of way.

For me, back-of-the-boat time means spending time in silence, in solitude, in prayer, listening to music (particularly jazz), reading (more short stories, poetry, and plays these days), writing, napping, exercising, sketching, computer gaming, and a few other activities. Such sanctified pleasures have come to matter as much to me as anything that I do in my vocational life as a preacher and teacher. In a most important way, I have come to understand that those pleasures *must* matter if I am to have any chance at all of doing ministry in good spirit and in full truth.

The sanctified pleasures of the back of the boat feed my personhood directly and unconditionally. They nurture my well-being from the inside out. They give more to me than they demand from me. Somewhere along the line, we have been led to believe that the ministerial life is all sacrifice. It is not. A vocation in ministry is so much more! The person inside of the minister cannot, and will not, live without unconditional acceptance and unmitigated delight. The back of the boat is a place where we may feel God's full acceptance and bask in the glorious joy that is life apart from our striving and straining. The back of the boat holds the key to personal wholeness and wellness, prerequisite ingredients for vital and vibrant ministry in our weighty and harried world.

A Prayer and Play Day

Eugene Peterson describes his sabbath, part of which he shares with his wife, as a day of prayer and play. I like these defining words—"prayer and play." I feel like I have had a good "day off" when it is been a day of being delightfully "on." I define "on" as being more alert to and thankful for my many blessings, and "on" in terms of doing things that "turn me on," things that are not about achieving but celebrating; not about producing but playing.

If I were limited to a single message of advice to aspiring pastors, it would be this: Set aside at least one day per week for prayer and play, or for the prayer of play. The drudgery that settles in on ministry during the third or fourth year (if not sooner) would be limited substantially or possibly eliminated if we clergy would observe this one act of grace for ourselves, for our families, and for our churches. And that is the empowering irony of stepping back from the giving and producing. Sabbath time actually energizes us for more creative involvement in every area of life.

I believe that observing a weekly sabbath has strengthened me as a husband, father, pastor, and professor. Moreover, sabbath helps me to have a healthy and holy appreciation of work. When I run and work nonstop, eventually I begin to feel negatively about the work that I so love. By so doing, I make an enemy of the work when the real enemy is an imbalance that does not allow time for respite—a backing away that yields perspective and potency for new engagement.

A fundamental problem of contemporary ministry is that we spend too much time emptying ourselves and not enough time being filled. This accounts for "the robe beneath the robe"—the robe of fatigue that too many clergy almost never take off. Sabbath is a fill-up day. It is a day to be renewed by remembering whose and who we are. It is a day to forget about responsibilities, tasks, calendars, deadlines, meetings, problems, and any other work-related issues that draw energy out of us. The sabbath focus ought be to receive energy, to have our souls filled with love for God and for life, for being's sake, for play's sake.

Here are a few ways you can ensure that your prayer and play day is just that. First, decide on the day of the week that suits you best; block out that day in your calendar and inform your congregation of the day you have chosen. Early in my ministry I tried observing Mondays for a sabbath. It didn't work out for me because I realized that I didn't feel fully relieved of ministry until late Monday afternoon. Though, perhaps wading more than swimming, I was still spending most of my time in the waters of ministry.

Second, tenaciously protect your prayer and play day. Only the most urgent of emergencies ought to postpone your sabbath. I used the word "postpone" because, when you miss your day for any reason, you should make it up. Honoring your day begins with you. One thing is certain: If you do not care enough to protect your time from unnecessary intrusions, interruptions will camp out at your door. The phone will ring; a wounded congregant will have to talk with you and only you; the meeting just won't be the same without you; and so forth. Believe that sabbath is as sacred as the Bible teaches. Experience the relief and rebirth of prayerful play. Become spoiled by it and hold on to your day like a child holding on to a favorite doll. To expand the analogy further, picture that doll as a person, and that person is you. Sabbath is about the sacred off/on time God has blessed us with in order to rediscover God and to recover ourselves.

Finally, make sure that you really pray and play on your sabbath. I understand prayer to be purposeful communion with God involving my verbal expressions—but even more deeply the nonverbal expressions of my heart, and deeper still, paying attention to the silence. My sabbath prayer life is less about my own words and more about my being empty, open, and receptive. Someone has said that one of the great maladies of our time is verbal intoxication. As wonderful as they are, too many words, especially those rendered within a short span of time, can be numbing. Nowhere is wordiness more of a liability than in our prayer lives. In my prayer life, particularly in my sabbath prayer life, I am committed to allowing for more empty spaces, for more pauses.

My wife once took me to see the great dancer Bill T. Jones perform. Later, reflecting on his amazing performance, I realized that the moments when he was not dancing were as important as the moments when he was moving so magnificently on stage. When he was at rest, I had the time to marvel at his last feat and to anticipate what he might do next. When we allow for verbal rest periods in prayer, space is opened up for us to appreciate God and to anticipate how God wants to move in our lives in the future.

My sabbath involves doing things just for the fun of it. I happen to enjoy reading, jazz, and computer games, especially flight simulators, strategy, sports, and adventure games. I have a growing interest in astronomy, chess, and sketching. Having a good time is one of the central gift-goals of sabbath.

There is a line from the movie *Chariots of Fire* that I will never forget. One of the long-distance runners says, "I believe God smiles when he sees me run." As a parent, it is not difficult for me to imagine God rejoicing in our delight because I get great satisfaction from seeing my children having a good time.

Necessary Losses

The title of a book written by Judith Viorst has never left me: *Necessary Losses*. The first essential loss for us all is that comfortable and protected place we call the womb. Many more losses follow, including relationships, places, and jobs. Life is a continuing cycle of losing and finding.

Getting to the back of the boat involves some painful, yet necessary losses. There are things that must be left behind, at least temporarily, if we are to experience the release and revival that comes from being in the back of the boat. What were some of the things Jesus gave up when he made his exit? He gave up being the central attraction. He gave up, at least for the moment, being responsible for what did and did not happen. (Give this up, and your ministry will be transformed for the better almost overnight.) He gave up the need to be present in order to ensure that things were being done and being done right. He gave up his multifaceted role as Jesus, the teacher, preacher, healer, and master, to be Jesus, the child of God.

My resistance to the reality of necessary loss manifested itself at the first church meeting I attended in which the moderator, not the pastor, had control of the proceedings. To be sure, I had looked forward to this meeting. It was a thrill to be the pastor of a church where I was not expected to carry the whole burden. I had found the declaration on the church's bulletin to be refreshingly true: "The ministers of this church are the people of the church." The meeting, I was assured, would further validate the church's strong lay leadership theology and practice. Sure enough, my sole responsibility at the meeting was the closing prayer. My report, like all the other reports, was reviewed, and I was not asked to expound upon it. During the short ride home, I noted two feelings inside of me. On one hand, I marveled that a church meeting could happen without me playing a major role. On the other hand, I mourned that a church meeting could happen without me playing a major role. I had to absorb the necessary losses of the need to be in control and the need to feel needed.

Getting to the back of the boat involves loss, but the losses are nothing compared to the gains. We may lose control and notoriety, but we gain respite and peace. We may lose portions of our roles, but we find our souls. By heading to the back of the boat, we discover that less is more.

Owning Your "Am-ness"

Miles Davis, the late legendary jazz trumpeter, is reported to have said, "I am not what I do. I do what I am." His words are a fundamental truth that we all should learn and lean toward. A phenomenal musician, Davis could step back and see that there was something even more significant about himself: he was a self. Moreover, his statement indicates that he was aware that self precedes talent—self-formed and self-fueled talent. Davis's own self-understanding was that his musical gift flowed out from who he was apart from his gift, from his personhood.

Often in ministry, we interpret things the other way around: our "doing-ness" precedes our "am-ness." The living fallout of this belief is feeling empty inside even though activity abounds. This emptiness is the pain of a starving soul, which cannot exist on works alone or on works disconnected from being. The human soul must be fed by a sense of self-satisfaction—a sense of gratitude and delight, not rooted in any external thing but grounded in the fact that self exists and that it is held and loved by God. Ironically and miraculously, the buoyed self becomes a revving engine of creative and inspired engagement. Such buoyancy cannot happen apart from a healthy connection to the self. Persistent creative engagement does not thrive in environs of self-deprivation.

When we cut ourselves off from self through overload and hurry, at best we become hollow producers of good works. We become chronic doers, simultaneously experiencing the equally chronic nagging and gnawing reminder that we are mysteriously and miserably unfulfilled. Chronic doing is the tragedy of valuing works over selfhood. It is the tragedy of failing to grasp the essential role that self-affirmation plays in the best form of self-actualization—sharing our talents and skills through doing. God never intended for ministry to supersede personhood; rather ministry is to *proceed out of* personhood. We do our best work when we are firmly rooted in who we are. To accent doing and neglect being is to wrongly live out both and to seriously undercut the sanctified totality of all that we do and all that we are.

CHAPTER FIVE

The Sacred Pace

A Pace of Peace

Something does not quite fit in the story about Jesus out on the boat with the disciples. The narrative seems to include contradictory data. Verse 38 indicates that Jesus was aroused from his sleep by a few of the frightened disciples. They woke Jesus up. But the beginning of verse 39 clearly reveals that Jesus awakened. The disciples did not awaken him; he got up on his own. Which was it?

I see two possible solutions. The first is that Jesus' awakening was one continuous motion that includes both the disciples waking him up and Jesus waking himself up in response to their initial prodding—not a far-fetched solution. After all, it happens every day in many homes. Sometimes we have to call our spouses, children, or houseguests several times before they wake up. They begin the process with the first appeal, but rarely does the first call engender an enthusiastic rousing from the bed—except, of course, in the case of children on Christmas morning!

Solution #2 also rings true to the natural ebb and flow of everyday life: namely, that the disciples *did* wake Jesus up, but Jesus turned over and went back to sleep. I remember doing this many times as a teenager during the long, fun days of summer. I had a job cleaning up at a large department store. At 6:00 A.M. or so, one of my parents would yell for me to get up, but often I would go back to sleep for fifteen or twenty *sweet* minutes and dutifully wake up on my own to get to work on time. I just needed to catch those last few "winks" of sleep.

Whatever the explanation for the apparent contradiction, there is a common message here related to self-care: *Jesus does not rush or hurry into action.* He moves at what I refer to as a *sacred pace—a living speed characterized by peace, patience, and attentiveness.* By peace, I mean an abiding sense that all is well. By patience, I mean activism with waiting inside of it. By attentiveness, I mean being thoroughly focused on the matter of the moment.

One of the alluring qualities in Jesus was his embodiment of serenity. His witness was all the more striking when it was set against a backdrop of exceedingly trying situations and circumstances. For example, there was the time when Jesus walked right through a crowd determined to throw him off of a cliff. His peace was not the absence of tension. I believe that Jesus agonized at times about things, just as we do. But the impression we get from Scripture is that somehow, some way, all tension was routed through Jesus' peaceful center, and therein was transcended and transformed.

Converging with Jesus' peace was his patience. Jesus could move out, when necessary, in a spirit of intense engagement. But just as important, he knew when and how to wait. He seemed to live by an inner thermostat that was set on "calm and deliberate." Jesus knew that attending to problems quickly did not solve them. Mohandas Gandhi is reported to have said, "There is more to life than increasing its speed."

Jesus' ministerial style stands in direct contrast to the ministerial styles of most. Rarely did Jesus move with great haste and all deliberate speed. The disciples found out on the boat that night that Jesus did not jump at every beck and call. His responses to the various demands and invitations placed before him were characteristically measured and patient.

The third quality of Jesus' sacred pace, attentiveness, is no less striking and important. Beset with issue after issue, Jesus had a way of focusing exclusively on what he was doing at the time. Once he brought that motion to its end, he moved on to the next matter, which then would become the recipient of his full focus. Even when he was interrupted, he did not divide his focus. He would transfer his full attention to the "interruption," and then return to the original matter, as in the case of the hemorrhaging woman (Luke 8:40-56). Jesus was already on an "emergency call," but his attention to the moment was so intense that he was able to feel the woman's intrusion, address it, and then return his focus to the call on hold.

I think the sacred pace of Jesus is a much-needed contrast to the prevailing ministry (or care-giving) style that has us (1) doing too much, (2) doing too much at one time, and (3) doing too much as fast as we can. This three-headed demon is driving many ministers and their spouses to early graves—emotionally and physically. We can be liberated by internalizing the peace, patience, and attentiveness demonstrated by Jesus.

The Spirit within the Stride

Howard Thurman relays a profound story that relates to our dashing lives:

> There is a story told of the musk deer of North India. In the springtime, the roe is haunted by the odor of musk. He runs wildly over hill and ravine with his nostrils dilating and his little body throbbing with desire, sure that around the next clump of trees or bush he will find musk, the object of his quest. Then at last he falls, exhausted, with his little head resting on his tiny hoofs, only to discover that the odor of musk is in his own hide.[1]

The source of Jesus' delight was his experience with God. Jesus evidenced peace, patience, and attentiveness because God inspired these things inside him. Unlike the musk deer, Jesus never rushed about seeking to fulfill one need after another, because he already had what he needed most—within himself. He never sought fulfillment from the outside in because he was constantly being filled from the inside out. He never dashed around seeking self-validation and gratification; he found these and more in fellowship with God. Through his intimacy with God, Jesus received that which we pursue through overload and hurry—meaning, joy, and serenity. The genuine manifestations of these realities are found inside us.

Controlling the Pace of Our Response

A fundamental fact about Jesus and the velocity at which he lived and ministered is that *he always seemed to be in control of the pace of his response to life.* He seemed to have a spiritual speedometer inside of him that did not allow him to move at a frantic, rash speed. He moved with deliberation and passion, which was all too apparent even in the most demanding of situations.

When he was faced with the death of Lazarus and the searing grief of Mary and Martha, Jesus entered fully into the loss and pain of death and grief; yet he did not allow the crisis of that grief to break his characteristic purposeful stride.

The tension was probably quite thick when Jesus was asked by a furious mob of religious leaders to sanction the stoning of a woman apparently caught in the act of adultery. Again, Jesus became fully involved in the crisis that confronted him, but he never allowed the crisis to get into him to the point of dictating a rushed and merely reactive response.

This internal pace thermostat control was operative most especially when Jesus was moving with a sense of urgency, like during the Last Supper and the conflict in Gethsemane. Even on the cross, at his weakest moment, Jesus seemed to be responding more to an internal spiritual beat than to the external physical pounding of the nails. A modern-day parallel occurs daily, even hourly, in hospital emergency rooms where doctors and nurses understand the necessity of practicing calmness and control, even in the midst of carrying out hastily executed medical procedures. If Jesus' pace-controlling ability was a useful skill in his time, enabling him to remain steady and mindful in perilous circumstances, it is an even more useful skill for us today.

A great deal of the overload we experience is directly related to our inability to control the pace of our responses to life in general, and ministry in particular. We live as if all invitations must be accepted; as if all responses must be made as soon as possible; and as if all matters must be resolved with all speed. The regulating, oppressive rhythm of our time is "more, more, more, faster, faster, faster!" The message Jesus sends us in the way that he handled the storm situation is as liberating as it is clear: *You have the power to control the pace of your response.*

Have you heard the saying "A person cannot ride your back unless it is bent"? People cannot run you ragged unless you let them. Institutions and organizations cannot weigh you down with expectations and deadlines unless you let them. Ministry cannot crush you into the ground unless you let it. You have the power to control the pace of your response to each and every request made of you. Stop blaming persons and circumstances for the overload in your life! Stop blaming the church or other organizations. Exercise your power to set boundaries, to say "no," and to live and labor at a sacred pace. If this is perceived as negligence related to your "responsibilities," then it is *sanctified negligence.*

The liberation that comes from setting the pace of our own response is dramatic. The underlying seismic shift is that we go from being externally driven to being internally driven. Too often we live captive to the demands of this modern age and the burdensome expectations of others. Marching to these tunes results in lives overly determined by external factors. Kevin Cashman says profoundly, "In [an] externally driven state of identity, life is fragile, vulnerable, and at risk. Everything that happens to us defines who we are. We become our circumstances. Life defines us."[2]

Embracing the power to control the pace of our response in any given situation is a way of loosening the death-grip of external influence. We may not have any power over how the winds blow, but we have the power to adjust our sails. This power of response/pace control is one of the most potent forces we wield as human beings. This force has carried persons through the most damning of circumstances. Their salvation was that no matter how horrific the evil that afflicted them, they held on tight to their power of response. Sometimes that response was harnessing the will to survive and even thrive against all odds.

Savoring Pace: My Sacred Pace

Toward the end of summer 1998, I felt myself grieving. The grief was more than simple regret that a time of more play and less labor was coming to a close. As I struggled to name what I was feeling, it dawned on me that what saddened me was the sense of impending loss. What I feared losing at summer's end was a more relaxed, peaceful, and patient living pace that I had fallen into—or that had fallen into me.

I noticed it when my wife and I went on a cruise to Alaska. A financial blessing made it possible for us to take the dream vacation we had talked about since the beginning of our marriage eighteen years prior. It was the trip that tripped me up in several life-giving ways.

First, I was awed by the vastness of the Gulf of Alaska, over which we traveled. I had seen great bodies of water before, from a distance, but for the first time in my life I was *in* a great mass of water for days. From our large window, I marveled at all the water. It didn't seem to end, and I thought that it was as deep as it was wide.

Second, the glaciers arrested me—towering masses that were not green or brown, but white and blue. Gliding into College Fjord, we were completely surrounded by sixteen ice-blue glaciers. Perhaps the most memorable vision of all for me was the streams rolling down the mountainsides. Not just seeing them, but hearing them brought me to extended pauses and complete stops. Louisiana, my home state, had not afforded me such sightings. While I had expected that the trip to Alaska would be an amazing one, I had not expected that it would move me in such profound ways.

As I thought about it more and more, I began to realize that my summer-ending grief was connected to Alaska in some way. It wasn't so much missing the special places, but the savoring pace—the pauses and the stops to which the places in Alaska continued to call me.

In calling me *to* something, Alaska was calling me *away* from something else. While on the cruise and in the wake of it, I began to sense that I was living life much too fast. To be sure, this was not the first time this idea had surfaced in my head and my heart. There had been times when I wished that I had completed my senior year of high school along with my class instead of rushing off to college to get a head start. I occasionally had concerns that earning a graduate degree in divinity at an accelerated speed might have had some down sides. There also were moments when I felt that the three productive pastorates I had been blessed to experience over fifteen years had simply whizzed by. And then there were those times when I had looked at one or all of our four children and thought, "Are they growing up too fast, or am I just not seeing the stages?"

Concern for the fast pace of my life had nagged at me for a very long time. On the Alaskan cruise and in its aftermath, the concern whispering inside of me became a full-fledged protest.

The first stage of the protest was the grief I began to feel about having to get back up to speed after having been slowed down in Alaska. The grief led to anger. I began to say to myself in various ways, "I will not go back to running and rushing through life! If life were meant to be lived on the run, then slowing down would not feel so good. A leisurely pace would not feel so refreshing and right, and I would not grieve so over the loss of it." The anger led to resolve, a decision to live life at what I call a savoring pace—*a speed that allows for thinking more deeply, listening more carefully, and seeing more clearly.*

I do not remember when I first coined for myself the phrase "savoring pace." However, I do remember that it was in response to feeling that what was bubbling inside of me needed expression in the positive "savor more," as opposed to in the negative "slow down." The difference in expression is important. It is the difference between the more profound understanding of peace as not being merely the *absence* of tension, but the *presence* of harmony and justice. Peace is not simply a negation of something; it is the active presence of something. Likewise, savoring pace is not just negating or minimizing life's hurried pace; it is the celebration of life and paying more attention to it.

In the final year of his terminal illness, actor Michael Landon was asked about the impact of his impending death. Specifically, he was asked if he loved his family more because he would soon be leaving them. Landon's thoughtful response was, "No, I can't say that I love them more. I've always loved them. I do notice them more." What a convicting response!

We go through so much of our lives barely noticing the people or things around us. After a while, we just accept the fact that the numbing drudgery that ensues is just the way life is. Oh, certainly there are moments of deep joy and periods of great satisfaction. But sadly, we reach a point—no, we drive ourselves to a point—where those moments are the exception and not the rule. Savoring pace is about making the knowing-that-you-are-thoroughly-alive moments the rule.

To savor is to taste or smell with pleasure, to relish, to delight in, to enjoy with pleasure. The word has its origination in the Latin *sapere,* which means both "taste" and "be wise." The connection between the physical and the psychological inherent in that root has never been more important. For me, the savoring is in the physical *slowing,* but just as much, it is in the revelatory *showing* within the slowing. Savoring pace yields the richer, brighter life that opens to us once we slow down enough to notice it more. Savoring pace challenges our frenzied pattern of *paying attention to more* with a gentle yet persistent appeal to *pay more attention.*

Keeping the Pace

I believe that the quality of my remaining earthly life will be greatly determined by how well I am able to pace the circumstances of my life. The late pastor/politician Adam Clayton Powell had a pet phrase, "Keep the faith, Baby." I have come to believe that savoring pace must be kept in much the same way, as in keeping it delightfully but tenaciously sustained. One of the reasons why we must intentionally and deliberately "Keep the pace, Baby" is a reality called *entrainment.*

In his book *Timeshifting,* Stephan Rechtschaffen defines entrainment as a "process that governs how various rhythms fall into sync with one another."[3] For example, if you were to place two out-of-sync pendulum clocks next to one another, guess what? In a short time, they would be exactly in sync. Rechtschaffen makes the case in his book that a comparable parallel reality holds true with persons in relationship with one another and with persons in relationship to institutions. We unconsciously catch up to (or slow down to) each other's pace; we fall in step with each other's stride. Thus, if everyone around you is moving fast, rarely resting and never stopping, the likelihood of you doing the same is inevitable unless you intentionally begin to live at a sacred, savoring pace.

An Act of Defiance

To live at a more savoring pace is to engage in an act of protest against the powers inside us that lead us to overload and hurry, and against the powers outside us, including overly demanding and overly hurried work settings. Many institutions, including religious ones, make demands on employees that lead to personal abuse and familial neglect. The legitimizing rationale is that sacrifice is necessary and that the bigger ends (often measured in dollars and cents) will justify the threatening means. When an employee's salary and advancement are based on adherence to unrealistic expectations, the situation is especially agonizing. People desire peace, but not necessarily at the expense of security and prosperity.

To practice savoring pace in a setting that thrives on overload, or that is in denial about it, is to go against the grain and risk all of the associated negative interpretations. You may be perceived as not being a team player; you may be thought of as a slacker. Other people, acculturated to an environment of overload and hurry, may regard you as disloyal. When Jesus arrived on the scene of Lazarus's death four days "late," he was accused of being responsible for his friend's death. Blame and accusation may come as a result of deciding that you cannot and will not do it all, and that you will not seek to do everything as soon as possible.

When faced with the dilemma of conflicting paces, you really have only two healthy options. One option is to remain on the job and responsibly satisfy institutional expectations within the boundaries of your own limitations. The other choice you have is to seek other employment. You may choose to work in a setting that values and encourages self-care more than your current context does—one that grasps the essential connection between institutional accomplishment and personal well-being.

Remember to give away your time and energy, but not your soul. And whatever your vocation and work environment, you must reserve time for yourself and for your own delight and growth. The fact is that you are helping those around you with your model of a healthy pace and reasonable limits. The demands of our overloaded living oppress others and contribute to the overall sense of mindless haste in the world. Living purposefully, while resisting overload and hurry, helps the world to right itself toward wholeness and well-being.

The Biggest Foe of All

There is another foe you must face and defy if you are to live at a savoring pace. This foe can be much stronger than any work setting, though it is much smaller. This foe is you. In listening to myself and others through the years, I have come to one big conclusion: *The greatest hindrance to eliminating overload is a mindset locked on measuring life solely in terms of production and speed.* More! More! Faster! Faster!

Many of us have been living this way for so long that it is hard to admit the negative effects of our life's pace, even when we are hurting all over. Moreover, we have been nourished by overload for so long that, in some ways, the overload has taken on a life of its own. Having been fortified inside of us through the years, the overload spirit now believes it has a right to exist, and it will not give up without a fight! It will struggle hard to remain a fixture in a life where it is firmly rooted, nourishing the need for acceptance and achievement. When challenged, it will point the finger at other life realities as the cause of such conditions as anxiety and depression. It may even dare to suggest that we have not done enough.

And then there is the slick trick that dupes us into believing that all is well. The overload spirit will pretend to give in to our demands for respite and play as if to say, "Okay, you got me." But the catch is that we will hear the voice of unfinished tasks teasing and taunting us throughout the supposed rest. All too often this rest is ended after only a couple days, just long enough for the needle of our internal energy indicator to move ever so slightly off "E." After this false rest we proceed to restart the engine of overloaded living and begin driving harder and faster than before to catch up on the work that has piled up. So much for the rest!

Hearing the Cry of the Neglected Voice Inside

I have journaled for the past fifteen years. It is my way of paying more attention to my life. In addition, I hash out the struggles of my heart and head by writing through them. During a recent sabbatical from teaching, I wrote in my journal even more. One day I felt a conversation welling up inside me between the self that had been "peaced" together through sabbatical and the self that wanted to get back to business as usual. I allowed my imagination to overhear a conversation between these two sides of me. To better facilitate my objective listening stance, I began taking notes of the cerebral conversation with my nondominant hand, my left hand. I wrote what I heard in my heart without stopping to edit or interpret what I was writing. Here is how the scribbled conversation in my journal reads:

> *Savoring Pace Voice (SPV):* I will speak first. I will not be suppressed any more. You have got to understand that you need me in order to live. Kill me off and you kill yourself. I am trying to save you. Please, let me!
>
> *Overload and Hurry Voice (OHV):* But there is still so much that I want to do. . . .
>
> *SPV: (interrupting with anger)* Stop it right there! Life is more than doing. You know that. It's time that you accept it—and do whatever you have to do to truly accept it. If you don't, you are going to lose it all. You are going to lose your soul.
>
> *OHV:* I didn't mean to. . . .
>
> *SPV: (interrupting with gentleness)* I know you didn't. . . . Don't feel guilty or ashamed or angry. That will just make matters worse. Just let me love you. I am your friend, not your enemy. You have to trust me.

I think that there is a self inside each of us that is tired of the violence we are inflicting on it. Again in the words of Fannie Lou Hamer, this weary and worn self is "sick and tired of being sick and tired." Martin Luther King Jr. heard that same self speaking in the trying days of the Montgomery Bus Boycott:

> Almost every week—having to make so many speeches, attend so many meetings, meet so many people, write so many articles, counsel with so many groups—I face the frustration of feeling in the midst of so many things to do [that] I am not doing anything well.[4]

Some part of each of us understands and even yearns for activity, but not at the expense of wellness. It is that self who speaks to us in those quiet moments, challenging us to slow down and stop carrying so much. Listen to that voice within, the neglected voice. It is trying to save you. Let it.

Setting the Pace: Welcoming the Day

Early morning is a good time for devotion, not only because of the quiet, the sunrise, and the freshness it affords, but also because it gives us an opportunity to welcome the day. In our overly busy world, days can spill over into each other. Evidence of this may surface when we have to think about what day it is before leaving a message on an answering machine or when we check the date before writing a check. Days and dates can easily lose their distinctiveness, and in some cases, their value. We innocently say, "T.G.I.F.! Thank God, it's Friday." What about the other days of the week?

One of the ways that you can savor the gift of days is by taking a moment to welcome each day. Before you begin working or even *think* about working, receive the day—a sacred invitation to life—with glad acceptance. If you can, gaze out a window and take in the scenery. Deeply inhale the air of a new day. You may want to light a candle or make some other small, but meaningful, gesture in honor of the new day.

By welcoming each day that comes, you are expressing gratitude for much more than time to get things done.You are declaring yourself awake and appreciative of the dialogues, the challenges, the explorations, and the surprises that each new day brings. By welcoming the day, you are signaling your desire to be cocelebrant and cocreator with God once more.

---

[1] Walter Earl Fluker and Catherine Tumber, eds., *A Strange Freedom* (Boston: Beacon Press, 1998), 310.

[2] Kevin Cashman, *Leadership from the Inside Out* (Provo, Utah: Executive Excellence Publishing, 1998), 23.

[3] Stephan Rechtschaffen, *Time Shifting* (New York: Doubleday, 1996), 21.

[4] David Garrow, *Bearing the Cross* (New York: William Morrow and Company, 1986), 99.

CHAPTER SIX

Savoring Pace Life-Lines

Savoring Pace Cards

I have found that if I am to be successful at resisting my own tendency toward overdoing and the cultural provocations to overdo, I must have daily practical helps. My savoring pace cards are an enormous help. I have about one hundred or so of these small cards, and each day I choose one to read and focus on living that principle throughout the day. As sayings come to me, I write them down and they become part of my "Savoring Pace Life-Lines." The following are a few of my favorite redeeming reminders, with a few lines of explanation.

Sign a Peace Treaty with Conditions You Cannot Control

Much of life's frustration results from fretting about things that are out of our hands, including the choices our loved ones make. As we become more at peace with the reality of being God's children and not God incarnate, anxiety escapes from us like air going out of a punctured tire. We are able to sign a "peace treaty" that allows us to coexist with situations we are unable to eradicate, fix, or otherwise control.

Comply with the "Law of Limited Do-ability"

There is a natural law that we insist on challenging and breaking: *We can never do all that needs doing.* In part, our devotion to the idol gods of adrenaline, achievement, and affirmation blinds us to the reality of this fundamental law. Also, we resist the law because, in our blindness, it seems that submitting to the law comes too close to slothfulness and negligence. In fact, the law of limited do-ability is a sacred one, helping to ensure that we will experience the fullness of life through being as well as doing. And just think about it for a moment: What would the ability to "do it all" do for you? Limitation is not the enemy; overload is.

Grace Yourself!

One of my father's favorite admonitions was, "Don't treat anybody any better than you treat yourself." The sad fact is that most ministers give whole loaves to others while settling for crumbs themselves. As you minister to God's children, don't leave out the child who is just as worthy as any child of God—you.

Climb the ALPS: God's Abiding, Loving Presence

My morning devotional includes several practices that tend to flow into one another: silence or quiet waiting, meditation, intercessory prayer, Scripture reading, journaling, poetry reading, other reflective reading, contemplation of art or music, and sketching. The practices do not follow any set order. At times, some practices receive additional emphasis and some things are left out. The connecting chord between all of the exercises is the fresh realization that I am loved by God unconditionally, as we all are. Climbing the mountain of God's love is a reminder that I am a child of God, a person whom God loves (as the Spinners once sang) with "a mighty love." Scaling the mountain means hearing with the freshness of the morning dew the call within to live and laugh and give and grow in God's love.

Joy Is an Inside Job

Although external factors greatly influence our lives, it is our internal response to external forces that makes or breaks us. This awesome response capability abides within each of us. One of the implications is that we have the power to regulate our own joy, our own feeling of soul-satisfaction with life. The choice is ours to curse the storm, to run for cover, or to sing in the rain.

Overdrive and Overload Are Death-senders

I was stunned when I first heard the confession, "It was easier kicking my drug addiction than it was kicking my addiction to alcohol." But, the ensuing explanation made all the sense in the world. The person speaking said the stigma associated with drug usage strengthened his resolve to become drug-free. However, because drinking is a socially accepted activity, he had less incentive to quit.

Overload and overdrive are acceptable modes of existence, yet we are distressed about how busy we are. Conversely, we display a measure of pride about having such packed schedules. (Some groups take twenty minutes or more to schedule the next meeting. Why? Because everybody is so busy.) Busyness remains a status symbol for success and accomplishment. Until we confess the deleterious effects of excessive activity, we will be unable to eliminate it from our lives. Overload is not a mild headache that we can relieve by taking a couple of pills. Overload is a serious illness that, if left untreated, can cause emotional and physical death.

Be True to Your Own Vision and Imagination!

High blood pressure has been dubbed "the silent killer" because many people succumb to it without ever knowing they had it. There are many quiet killers, including that of not being who we really are. We tend to spend too much of our time trying to live out scripts written by or for other people. Beginning in childhood, we lose precious moments transforming ourselves into the false images that people construct for us. Moreover, we squander enormous amounts of energy trying to maintain these false images. What rest, what release, what peace there can be found in learning to be and loving who we are: one of God's splendidly unique children.

Cassandra Wilson, the great contemporary jazz vocalist, revealed the conversation in which she came to terms with her need to step into herself:

> I was on the path of imitation, wanting to sound exactly like [noted jazz singer] Betty Carter. Wanting to be that. Nothing was more important than [legendary saxophonist] Charlie Parker. And [Steve

> Coleman] said to me, "Well, that's true: Charlie Parker is very important. But who are you?" And that was the beginning, really for me in New York, the beginning of thinking about what my contribution was going to be. What's my expression going to be like?[1]

Jazz trumpeter Fats Navarro, gone too soon at the age of twenty-six, once said, "I'd like to play a perfect melody of my own, all the chord progressions right, the melody original and fresh—my own."[2] As you follow your vision, do not depend excessively on the path being cleared for you. Remember the Ashanti proverb: "Do not follow the path. Go where there is no path and begin the trail." And, as Søren Kierkegaard reminds us, "Be that self which one truly is."

Watch Out for the Rainbows

It was one of those serendipitous moments that make a person thrilled just to be alive. I was talking with a colleague at Andover Newton Theological School about a class we were coteaching. Our hallway conversation ended with us sharing some matters of vocation and calling. I told her that I was nearing the "sweet spot" of feeling that a work that appeared to be greatly needed was also a work I was beginning to truly want to do. Calling was intersecting with passion in my life. She smiled as I headed to my office, and there it was. Outside my office window was one of the most beautiful rainbows I had ever seen. I yelled out to my colleague, "Come back in here, quick!" We both enjoyed that rainbow, which I had received as a divine exclamation point to the vocational harmony I was experiencing.

Each New Day Is Seeing You Play for the First Time

A major league baseball player was asked how he could play every game with great intensity. This star of the diamond gave a jewel of a response: "I imagine that every time I go out on the field, there is someone in the stands who is watching me play for the first time."

If we are not careful, we may lose our zest for life by allowing days to run into each other in a blur of rushed activity. Take time to greet each day. Remember that each is a day uniquely holy and good on its own merits. It is neither yesterday nor tomorrow; it is today. Each day deserves the best you can offer it because it has never seen you play. Ellen Langer offers wise advice in this regard:

> People who are waiting to live put off today in exchange for tomorrow: "As soon as the children are grown, I'll..."; "After the business matures I can...." "Once the application is finished, I'll...." Work and play are states of mind. We won't learn that as long as we think we should delay gratification. Waiting is mindless. It suggests that there is no way to enjoy what is being done at the moment.[3]

Scripture says it this way: "This is the day that the Lord has made. Let us rejoice and be glad in it!"

Live like Duke Ellington Celebrated Music

Extraordinary bandleader, pianist, and composer himself, Edward Kennedy "Duke" Ellington's highest accolade for personal skill and contribution was to say that the artist was "beyond category." In the estimation of many, Ellington himself was that and more. Ellington was music, particularly jazz, personified. He was a walking note, composition, and song. His love of music was illustrated once on an airplane. He asked one of the members of his renowned band for some composition paper since his own had been packed with his baggage. When the band member said that he had none, Ellington took off his coat, sat down, and began writing the musical idea that was burning inside him on his white shirtsleeve!

Feeding Ellington's abiding passion were two realities open to all of us. First, Ellington was constantly learning and expanding. Perhaps journalist Stanley Crouch articulated that quality in the artist best: "Ellington didn't stop creating. He seemed incapable of settling for an older version of himself."

The second reality was Ellington's deep sense of loving acceptance, imparted to him especially by his mother, Daisy Ellington. She said to him often, "Edward, you are blessed. You don't have anything to worry about. Edward, you are blessed."[4]

Befriend the fire inside you and the forces that ignite its flame. Thrust yourself into the positive passion stirring inside. Let it bring you to the high places of creative expression and living joy.

Live like Johnny Hodges Played the Saxophone

Duke Ellington's legendary band was comprised of some members who had remained for well over thirty years. One of those long-time members, Johnny Hodges, was a star attraction in the band. His solos were a highlight of the band's musical portfolio. Think delicate, mellow, sweet, and seamless, and you have the style of Johnny Hodges. With Hodges, every note mattered; every note deserved equal attention. Moreover, he became so proficient with his musical gift that he made it look easy.

Good living is found in the details. Life, sweet and soulful, is not so much about paying attention to more, but paying more attention. As we take more time with small things, they add up to fulfillment, the likes of which we have never experienced before. We may become so devoted to such living that it will come naturally to us.

Live like Ella Fitzgerald Sang

That Saturday evening my sermon was not complete, and I didn't feel like finishing it. In fact, I didn't feel like doing much of anything. For some reason, I found myself playing a CD by a jazz vocalist I had heard of, but never paid much attention to. For the next fifty minutes or so, I was enraptured by a voice that touched my heart and lifted my spirit. Ella Fitzgerald was one of the select persons who Duke Ellington said was "beyond category." Her voice was clear, nimble, and filled with delight. Known as "the first lady of song," Fitzgerald sang each song as if she were singing it for the last time.

Though humble, I suspect that a great deal of her power came through the confidence she placed in her voice. She sang so beautifully because she sang so freely. Unshackled and reaching for the stars is not only the way to sing; it is the way to live!

You Can Play through Adversity

It was an outdoor performance and the phenomenal jazz tenor saxophonist was nearing the end of one of his inspired elongated solos. Suddenly, Sonny Rollins leaped from the edge of the stage. He landed badly and fell about three or four feet to the surface below. Just as suddenly as he fell, the music stopped. The sidemen on piano and drums ceased their playing. The trombonist set aside his instrument. The camera panned to Rollins lying prostrate and motionless on the ground.

It was one of those moments when no one knew what to do next. Then something amazing happened. Rollins nonchalantly crossed one leg over another and began to play a sweet soulful melody. The musicians exploded in laughter and amazement. What had transpired had not been rehearsed. The audience was awed, overcome with wonder and delight. Never before had they seen anything like it. As for Rollins, he kept playing, his back supported by Mother Earth. His saxophone was lifted to the sky, either oblivious to the fact that he had just broken his heel or knowledgeable of his injury but caught up in the miracle of playing through his pain.

Some suffering in life renders us motionless, such as that caused by severe and earth-shattering physical ailment or emotional trauma. Often, all we can do in the face of such assaults is nothing. Yet there are other painful realities wherein we may not be completely powerless—for instance, points of transition in our relationships with people or in our vocational pursuits. Perhaps these are the kinds of hardships that we can, if we are of a stronger mind, choose to play through.

Playing, journeying, and "joying" on, especially through adversity, is one of the most fulfilling and transcending experiences of all. The fulfillment is due, in part, to the defiance it births. Choosing not to let pain get the better of us and living by that choice can be invigorating and empowering, especially for persons in dire need of self-victory. Then there is the fulfillment of discovery. There is a kind of music, a deeper life experience that is realizable only through being rebelliously cheerful when life throws us to the ground. There are wondrous notes and chords in the music of life that can only be played or heard in the places where we suffer.

Use Your Power to Choose Peace

On that morning I awakened to a storm of concerns. Before my feet hit the floor, I began to think about one challenge after the next—including a large financial concern, strategies for improving my teaching that day, and the needs my children had raised the night before. All of these and more caused me to get up feeling weighted down. On top of it all, I began to feel guilty for not practicing what I preached. One of my sermons had challenged hearers not to be destroyed by "morning worry" before welcoming "morning glory." Well, that morning the worry was besting the glory—that was, until I remembered something else I had preached to others: You have the power to experience peace in any situation, no matter how trying the situation may be.

In that moment, I decided to live my own rhetoric, deliberately and intentionally. I went downstairs, sat down, and with quiet force, emptied my mind of all anxious thoughts. At first it was difficult, and the challenges were contrary. But, little by little, I began to feel more at ease. The more at ease I felt, the more at ease I wanted to feel. I found myself leaning into it, like a child stretching for a drink at a tall water fountain. Before long, I felt complete relief and release.

Though I had experienced such peace amid calm before, this time it was extra special because I was deliberate about making my own peace that morning and I consciously observed the process in motion. I am convinced that day was rerouted from a stressful one to a joyful one by accessing my power to choose peace.

Each of us has this power. I believe it is God-given and God-inspired. The implications are earth shattering. Since we have the power to choose peace, we have the capacity to survive, and even thrive, in life's tough places. In the words of the Negro spiritual, "Ain't that good news?"

Claim Your Calm

Periodically, long lists of names appear in newspapers across the country. The persons identified are either owed money or other items of worth by the state or federal government, or they are heirs to an estate. All of these persons have one thing in common: They hold verifiable rights to portions of wealth that they either do not want, or more probably, they do not know about.

There is a deep soul peace to which we are entitled as children of God. This peace defies understanding because it can hold itself, and hold the one who holds it, even under the most trying conditions. This peace has God's heart as its reservoir, still mysteriously sustained and strong through incalculable pain.

This soul peace, a bottomless calm of mind and heart, is ours. But first we must stake our claim to it. We must claim our calm, and keep claiming it over and over again.

We may do this each day by spending extended morning and evening moments, as well as more abbreviated moments throughout the day, reminding ourselves that no matter what, all is and all will be well—really.

Check Your Pace

I am committed to keeping the savoring pace because I believe it to be a more sacred pace. I believe that Jesus' sacred pace was one of the keys to his dynamic spiritual strength. I believe that if I keep the sacred savoring pace, the sacred savoring pace will keep me.

For me, keeping the pace means checking my pace each day, throughout the day. I do this by taking a deliberate moment to notice what I am doing at the time, and how fast I am doing it. In the beginning, this was a tedious and somewhat distracting chore. However, staying with it has entrenched an alternative rhythm inside me more deeply each day. I no longer have one speed: faster. I now have another pace—a slower, more thoughtful savoring pace that I find far more satisfying, joyful, and productive.

Along the way, I have discovered many instruments for measuring my pace, including the following version of the Twenty-third Psalm by Toki Miyashina:

The Lord is my pacesetter, I shall not rush.
he makes me stop and rest for quiet intervals,
He provides me with images of stillness

which restore my serenity.
He leads me in ways of efficiency,
through calmness of mind,
and his guidance is peace.
Even though I have a great many things to
accomplish this day,
I will not fret,
for his presence is here
His timelessness,
His all-importance will keep me in balance.
He prepares refreshment and renewal
in the midst of my activity
by anointing my head with the oil of tranquility,
My cup of joyous energy overflows.
Surely harmony and effectiveness shall be the fruits of my hours,
for I shall walk in the pace of my Lord,
and dwell in His house forever.

I have two other ways to check my pace, not just in terms of evaluating where I am, but in terms of intentionally slowing myself down. First, I have developed a fondness for poetry. Ministers would do well to read poetry for the insight it yields into the power of words. Mark Twain is reported to have said "The difference between the right word and the wrong word is the difference between lightening and a lightening bug." Good poetry is delightful, undisputed proof of Twain's words. Yet beyond the benefit of enhancing our awareness, appreciation, and application of words, poetry can help nurture a more patient speed inside us. I do not believe that a person can read poetry fast and be blessed by it. Poetry, more than any other form of literary expression, begs for slow reading. Reading poetry carefully and patiently in the morning and at other points throughout the day helps to me to develop a more careful and patient style of living.

The other method of checking my pace that has greatly enhanced the way I live is listening to music. I have always appreciated music, gospel and rhythm and blues, in particular. Though I was born in the birthplace of jazz, it has been a late entry into the journal of my musical preferences. But, oh, what wonders it has brought! I listen more intently and carefully to jazz more than any other music style because of its great creativity and variety.

When I listen to other forms of music, I am carried away by the song's message or sustained rhythm and melody. When I listen to jazz, however, I slow down my listening to more fully appreciate the precipitation of diverse sounds and combinations. For example, one of the things I enjoy most is comparing how different artists present a particular song; for instance how Mary Lou Williams and Diane Schuur handle "Somewhere Over the Rainbow," or how a procession of artists musically massage Duke Ellington's "I Got It Bad and That Ain't Good."

Simply put, I don't just listen to jazz. I taste jazz. I savor jazz! I believe that savoring jazz has had a resurrecting ripple effect on my life. I find myself taking more time to enjoy life more thoroughly, including relationships, learning experiences, and surprises—those holy, unplanned intrusions that we would all do well to notice more.

Refer to Appendix B for information on ordering Savoring Pace Life-Lines.

---

[1] Cassandra Wilson, "A Sisterhood of Spirit," interview by Larry Blumenfield, *Jazzis*, June, 1999, 47.

[2] Fats Navarro, "Goin to Minton's," album notes. The Atlantic Group. (New York: Savoy Jazz, 1999).

[3] Ellen Langer, *Psychology Today*, March-April, 2000, 26.

[4] Jana Tull Steed, *Duke Ellington* (New York: Crossroad, 1999), 31.

CHAPTER SEVEN

Being Still

Speaking to a Storm

As ministers, we all would like to identify with Jesus on the boat that night. What daring! We only can imagine what it would be like to stand on the bow of the boat and speak to the tempest, the storm with an earthquake quality. Many of us enter ministry with a desire to make that kind of difference in the lives of people, especially when they are going through the trying storms of life. Though we would be like Jesus, the fact is that we are more suited for a role as one of the fearful disciples on the boat that night. Sure, we have our moments of bravery, but a great deal of our lives is spent living under the inhibiting clouds of doubt and fear.

If the events that night were to be performed on stage, perhaps the role that most of us could play without much rehearsal at all would be the storm itself. Yes, the storm. Most of us are walking storms, personal winds and waves of busyness, moving from one thing to the next with little or no time for respite.

Imagine yourself as the storm Jesus addressed that night. See and feel the strong gusts of busyness and haste that are inside of you—that have become you. For a moment, envision the countless tasks you have scheduled today as a great wave of overload. Do you see yourself? Can you feel the tornado churning inside of you? Can you hear the sound of the crashing waves of demand and expectation that others place on you, and that you place on yourself? As your fierce rampage continues, imagine yourself hearing a voice from within your own rage. It is a voice that breaks into your pandemonium, daring to demand that you observe "Peace"—that you "Be still!" Can you?

A Saturday Morning Grief Storm

Saturday mornings are a special time for me because they are especially conducive to back-of-the-boat experiences. On Saturdays, traffic on our street is minimal; usually there are no pressing responsibilities, and I am still in the residual calm of my sabbath the day before. But one Saturday was different. When I sat down, I realized that I didn't feel at peace; indeed, I was agonizing inside. Wanting to get some sort of handle on things, sporadically I began to write down what I was feeling. I began to relive some experiences from that week, including my participation in a very intense class on race relations in America. The night before we had seen a movie that portrayed, simply but powerfully, deeply entrenched racial barriers in our nation. The turmoil churned out of class and cinema had remained inside of me. I was grieving racism: grieving how our children must be challenged to do better than their forebears; how the church is often more of a taillight than a headlight on racial justice; how necessary social gains will mean unavoidable personal pains.

As I sat with my own pain and perturbation that morning, I began to make an effort to halt the surge of all thoughts about racial conflict, about any kind of conflict, about anything period. Steadily, I began to receive the peace of the morning in its *busy-less* beginning. After a few moments of mentally holding the realities that had created a twister of tension inside me at bay, I found myself feeling the deep cool refreshment of mental and spiritual peace.

Making and Holding Peace

The Hebrew understanding of peace includes wholeness and well being. Peace is not merely the absence of conflict, but the presence of godly serenity and, as Christians believe and teach, the presence of Christ. As for

Jesus, he made two striking observations regarding peace that we do well to remember.

On the occasion of his Sermon on the Mount, Jesus said, "Blessed are the peacemakers," signaling that peace involves the acquiescence of our hearts and the action of our bodies. We cannot simply wish peace into existence; we must be cocelebrants with God in *affirming* and *claiming* peace, both within and without. Notice that I did not use the term "establishing." It is splendidly hopeful and wonderfully encouraging for us to remember that our peacemaking is not concocted from scratch. Since peace is godly, peacemaking has more to do with uncovering what is there already, with working to open our spiritual eyes to what is already in front and inside. Peacemaking is a less daunting enterprise when we realize that the peace we seek is, in a very real sense, already made. Going through layer upon layer of ignorance and fear in order to transcend into existing peace more accurately reflects the human challenge.

The other statement Jesus made regarding peace occurred during the stormy weather that night as he and the disciples stood on the bow of the boat. Jesus told the storm to be at peace, to "be still." In the Greek, Jesus was telling the storm to "muzzle itself," to hold its energy inside itself and to bring its turbulence to a place of rest. Amazingly, the storm *did* muzzle itself, bringing peace to all of its surroundings, including the fearful disciples. With his command to the storm, Jesus emphasized the capacity for peace to be observed through an internal holding, or muzzling of energy.

The striking reflection here is that the power to affirm a state of calm lies within the storm itself. The storm has the ability to diffuse its own rage. It is within the storm's capacity to have peace if it will restrict its own energy, which is raging out of control. The key is that the storm must believe in and execute its potential to calm itself, to hold itself within itself. Implied here is more than just a momentary action, but continuous action—to get calm and keep calm.

Peace is not just something we affirm through our awareness of and commitment to a divinely granted serenity in our world. Peace is something we experience, with God's help, through holding the raging tensions within. This was my experience on that unforgettable Saturday morning. Peace came when I took my feelings of grief and anger about racism and held them, not in the sense of denying their existence, but held in the sense of denying their power to rage uncontrollably inside of me. I held them in the sense of holding them up to the peace of God, which passes all understanding.

Letting Peace Make Us

After I held my peace that morning, once again I felt more hopeful than fearful in my spirit. I felt like going on. Peace of mind had given me fresh resolve. That experience led me to what I believe is a living connection between what Jesus told the multitudes about *making* peace that day, and what he told the storm about *holding* its peace that night. Namely, we stand a better chance of making peace in our world outside if we can hold peace in our world on the inside. We will become better at making peace when we become better at holding peace; in other words, when we become better at *letting peace make us.*

We let peace make us a little more each time we exercise the power already inside us to hold the storm in. We let peace make us when we seek the calm center that is at the eye of every storm. We let peace make us when we are no longer unconsciously dependent on the rush of crises, and when we are more consciously thirsty for the peace of God. Each incremental effort at holding our storms has a cumulative effect. Being made by peace slowly and regularly makes us peaceful persons. The more peaceful we are, the better peacemakers we become.

The Tone of His Voice

Many of us were blessed to have parents or guardians who loved us enough to challenge us. They loved us enough to speak loud and hard during those times when they perceived that we were living irresponsibly or when they felt our lives were in danger. Love not only whispers; love shouts when shouting is the most loving thing to do. If a loved one, or anyone for that matter, were about to be struck by a car, the observer would not whisper, "Get out of the way!" If a house is on fire, a bystander does not gently request that the occupants consider vacating the premises. The gravity of a situation causes genuine concern to amplify its voice.

Further encouragement to resist stormy living (overload and hurry) may be found by paying attention to the tone of Jesus' voice. The sudden squall was a storm of mammoth proportions that had the power to drown every last one of them. Recognizing the seriousness of the situation, Jesus responded by rebuking the storm. He did not request that the storm subside. He did not reason with it about the wisdom of stopping. He did not plead with it to cease. Jesus *commanded* the storm to "Be still!"

You may think that hurry and overload are simply necessary drawbacks of ministry. You may think that chronic fatigue is just part of the price ministers pay for being faithful. You might think that Jesus intended ministry in his name to be more drudgery than delight. If you have had any of these thoughts, listen again. Listen to the tone of his voice on the boat. Listen to his deeply felt concern for your peace and well-being, and for the peace and well-being of your family. Hear his sacred intolerance for that which is threatening you, harming you, or causing you to be afraid. Is Jesus overreacting to the storm's presence, or does the severity of his tone match the seriousness of the situation?

Noted preacher and pastor James Forbes tells of dreaming one night that he was attending a funeral. During the dream, he realized that the funeral was his own. Just as the top of the casket was about to be brought down over his corpse, he began to shout, "I object! I object!" In the same way, we must vehemently protest and resist the overload that threatens to bury us prematurely!

One of the members of my church shared with me a story about the time she stood up to a snake. While just a schoolgirl in her native Nigeria, one day the alarm rang, signaling a possible air raid. All of the children made their way to the underground tunnel. As the students progressed further into the underground shelter, some of them began throwing rocks at a snake. Suddenly, the snake sprang up and positioned itself to strike. That is when young Flora stepped forward and commanded the snake, "Back away, in the name of Jesus!" The other children watched, stunned, as the snake obediently slithered away. For weeks, Flora said, students referred to her as "In the Name of Jesus." For sure, Flora's power surge was in the *name* she called, and the *manner* in which she called the name. She didn't gently urge the snake to leave; she *commanded* it to depart.

Jesus objected to the storm that night, just as he objects to our stormy ways of living and ministering. He knows that we are dealing with matters of life and death. Listen for your own good: Jesus is not asking that we be still; he is making a demand. Stillness is not an option for living and vocational wellness; it is a requirement.

Mental Stillness

The fact is that we practice physical stillness in small ways throughout the day. A child is encouraged to be still as a parent seeks to gently lift the splinter out of her fingertip; a bridal party remains still at the bequest of a photographer intent on getting the best shot possible; motorists are conditioned to pause at the appearance of the red sign with the four letters written in white, "S-T-O-P." We practice physical stillness in small matters and in matters that may mean the difference between life and death.

One of the greatest challenges of our time is to understand the value of stillness to our mental health. When I say *mental stillness,* I am referring to a resting of the mind. Our overloaded and overdriven lives are manifestations of our overloaded and overdriven minds. Most of the time, we are thinking about multiple weighty matters, successively if not simultaneously.

In his marvelous book *Take Your Time: Finding Balance in a Hurried World*, Eknath Easwaran repeats the words of a wise teacher, Maher Baba: "A mind that is fast is sick. A mind that is slow is sound. A mind that is still is divine."[1] For his part, Easwaran compares the tyranny of a restless mind to television:

> Imagine that the mind is a kind of television with thoughts constantly changing channels. In this case, though, the remote control device is out of our hands; the mind is changing channels on its own. Sometimes when a thought succeeds in holding our attention, the mind actually settles on a particular show. At other times,

> when speeded up, the mind is racing through split-second shots like a frantic rock music video.[2]

Some rock music enthusiasts may object to Easwaran's analogy, but his point is clear enough: Overdriven minds detract from human wellness and wholeness. Although entrainment to the fast pace of our technological age is undoubtedly a chief inducement of our mental/emotional frenzy, it is merely an explanation, not justification.

"A Mind Is a Terrible Thing to Waste" is the oft-cited creed of the United Negro College Fund, yet ignorance is not the only way that we waste our minds. We may waste our minds by subjecting them to ceaseless pressure. It was not until years later that I fully understood the value of the advice my mother often gave me as a young man. In the middle of my academic paper-writing pushes, she would peer into the room and remind me, "Son, give your mind some rest." Our mental and emotional health depends on a rhythm of engagement and rest. To get out of sync is to risk the lethargic death of mindlessness. One of the most profound psychiatric pronouncements ever made is found in the Book of Proverbs, "For as he thinketh in his heart, so is he . . ." (Proverbs 23:7, KJV). I believe this text refers to the human thought process in the fullest sense: *what* we think (load), and *how* we think (pace).

A legendary pianist was once asked, "How do you handle the notes as well as you do?" The artist responded, "I handle the notes no better than any others; but the pauses . . . . Ah! That is where the art resides."

There is not only great art in the pauses, but great calm and strength as well. Practice the pauses in your life.

---

[1] Eknath Easwaran, *Take Your Time* (New York: Hyperion, 1994), 59.

[2] Ibid., 59-60.

CHAPTER EIGHT

The Stillness within the Stillness

Spiritual Stillness

There is a stillness within the stillness, a silence within the silence, and a breath within the breath. Silence and solitude, which mediate a heightened awareness of God's loving presence, are how I define spiritual stillness. Our need for spiritual stillness does not mean that we cannot experience God intensely amid the rigor and activity of life. On the contrary, maturing spirituality is about living out of an abiding God-consciousness. One is as likely to keenly sense God's grace while working as one is while playing or resting.

Tilden Edwards refers to this ongoing God intimacy as living with a "spiritual heart:" The spiritual heart is the true center of our being. It is the placeless place where divine Spirit and human spirit live together.[1] Spiritual stillness is about being more at home with the spiritual heart.

The spiritual stillness of which I speak is often unintentionally blocked by religious practices that can obstruct as much as they can enhance. For instance, prayer—experienced as mere monologue with God—can be a form of avoiding God. We often end up talking ourselves out of God's presence. Maybe this is what Madeline L'Engle was referring to when she said, "We build churches which are the safest possibles places in which to escape."[2] We also can dodge God under the guise of devotion by reading and singing, without leaving openings for stillness and silence. We may go from song to song, and Scripture to Scripture, without ever taking time to absorb, to sit, to wait, to question, or even to doubt.

Have you ever been in a room with someone yet not really noticed them? This is often the scenario in our jam-packed devotional times. It is possible to talk, read, sing, and think and never notice God, never give God an opening to speak or to simply and miraculously be with us.

A few years ago, I came across the strangest advice I had ever read in the introduction of a book: "When you are brought to silence, this book will be your enemy. Get rid of it."[3] The late Anthony De Mello wrote those words at the beginning of *Wellsprings: A Book of Spiritual Exercises.* When I first read De Mello's work, I didn't have the foggiest notion what the author meant. But one day I read the following words, attributed to Andrew Murry, and I finally understood what De Mello was saying:

> Take time to be separate from all friends and all duties, all cares and all joys; time to be still and quiet before God. Take time not only to secure stillness from [people] and the world, but from self and its energy. Let the Word and prayer be very precious; but remember, even these may hinder the quiet waiting. The activity of the mind in studying the Word, or giving expression to its thoughts in prayer, the activities of the heart, with its desires and hopes and fears, may so engage us that we do not come to the still waiting on the All-Glorious One. Though at first it may appear difficult to know how thus quietly to wait, with the activities of mind and heart for a time subdued, every effort after it will be rewarded; we shall find that it grows upon us, and the little season of silent worship will bring a peace and a rest that give a blessing not only in prayer, but all day.[4]

Quiet waiting, still waiting, silent worship—suddenly I knew what De Mello meant. I have not thrown his book away, but his point has found a home in my heart. Being quiet in God's presence is a powerful and underused devotional expression. Some traditional religious groups, such as the Quakers, have always prioritized quiet; many other traditions have not. While I thank God for my own black church tradition, I realize that my experience in that tradition had few moments of precious silence. While I still enjoy the oral and musical volume and energy of my root religious tradition, I am grateful to have it yoked with worshipful expressions that, though quiet, are no less revealing of God's loving grace and mercy.

To observe spiritual stillness is to recline in a uniquely, blissful place within the wide expanse of our relationship with God. There are two distinguishing marks of this dimension of our relationship with God: fearlessness and receptivity.

God-Fearlessness

I think James Washington is right when he says "We are afraid of God." Maybe this is the unconscious reason behind all of our doing and running: We are afraid that if we stop too long, we might see something, hear something, and feel something that will overwhelm us. Spiritual stillness is about daring the silence, standing up to it, and remaining within it long enough to experience God differently, if not more deeply.

Just two years after my father's passing, I discovered that remembering was a powerful way for me to experience his life after death. Some of my most precious memories are of those times when he drove me back and forth to Union Baptist Theological Seminary in New Orleans, the school where I began my formal theological studies as a teenager. During the trip, we would engage in general conversation. I remember laughing with him about humorous incidents, both in and out of the classroom. Most of all, I remember being with him one-on-one for at least thirty minutes a day. Our time together, engaging in verbal and nonverbal communication, nurtured familiarity, comfortability, and sensitivity that only grew through the years. Intimacy with God is nurtured through much the same way—being with God in simple, yet mysterious ways. For that reason and others, we must resist our rarely discussed but ever-present fear of such intimacy.

Without a doubt, Jesus' fearless relationship to God was a defining mark of his personality. It must have been striking to his followers that Jesus was so comfortable being alone with God. A time of silence and solitude was part of his daily regimen. Moreover, his stillness was portable, allowing Jesus to observe spiritual calm in the midst of trying circumstances. Spiritual stillness is about meeting our fear of God head-on, and having it melt away by daring to be in the presence of the holy One.

An essential component of our relationship to God is the sacred admonition spoken several times at both the birth and resurrection of Jesus. It may be the most repeated phrase in angelic pronouncements to persons; it is the whispered refrain of sunrise and the majestic appeal of sunset—*"Don't be afraid."*

Glad Acceptance

One morning, midway through my quiet time, it began to rain. At first, I thought the sound I heard was a rush of wind. But the sound of nature's applause continued, proving to be an early morning rain shower. In spite of the New England winter, I cracked my window to hear the sound more clearly. In my spirit, I began to receive the rain—to welcome it into my heart and soul. I felt a moment of inner refreshment that is beyond description. Then it dawned on me that whether or not it rains on the outside every day, we all need rain on the inside every day. Every day we need to receive the outpouring of God's unconditional love.

Duke Ellington ended his concerts by telling the audience, "Remember, we love you madly." We need to remember, or some of us may need to learn, that God loves each and every one of us madly.

One of the fundamental flaws in our interpretation of pastoral ministry is that we think our first and last task is offering. We pour out ourselves in service to God, church, and society. Although we are servants indeed, the first task of ministry is not to serve, offer, or give anybody anything. The first act of vocation in general, and ministry in particular, is to receive God's grace and acceptance. I believe this is what Jesus did when he took off on those early morning jaunts into the mountains. One of the secrets to the power of Jesus' ministry, I think, was that he remained receptive to God's loving attention.

Think about it: For the first nine months or so of our lives, we are in a fixed posture of receptivity. We are not required to exert any energy, to perform any function, or to meet any demands. Our sole embryonic calling in the comfort of our mother's womb is to receive nourishment. The crucial first act of life is the act of acceptance. As life proceeds and we assume the role of giver, our ability to receive remains an indispensable requirement for healthy, balanced living.

Glad acceptance is a form of spiritual inhaling. We would not live long if our bodies did not inhale oxygen. Breathing is a rhythm of taking in and letting go. Both actions are mutually dependent and essential. If there is no inhaling, then exhaling cannot occur, and vice versa. In ministry, we tend to exhale more than we inhale. We are constantly giving, and rarely genuinely receiving. Our ministries get winded, and we are chronically out of breath spiritually and often enough physically as well. The root meaning of the word *spirit* in Hebrew is movement of air, breeze, wind, and breath. Not to inhale in ministry, not to receive gladly, is tantamount to doing ministry without the Spirit. We are trying to do God's work without God. No wonder many ministers, and countless others in helping professions, often feel tired and empty inside.

To receive first and continuously places ministry in a radically and delightfully new perspective. In the first place, we begin ministry from a posture of fullness as opposed to emptiness. So many of us are accustomed to a life and ministry with our fuel gauge near or on "E," that it is hard to even conceptualize functioning in any other mode. We think that living in a state of exhaustion is normal. We accept that chronic fatigue goes with the territory; that it is just one of the vicissitudes of ministry. This is a lie! God never intended for the gospel of wholeness to be delivered by messengers who are drowning in brokenness. Spiritual stillness is a time to experience wholeness from the inside out; a time to receive the love, grace, and peace that we offer to others.

Second, beginning ministry in a posture of receiving gives us a heightened sense of levity in our giving, having first been the recipients of God's unconditional grace and goodness. Since God is a God of love and the gospel is a message of glad tidings of great joy, how do we account for the misery that seems to shroud the faces of far too many clergy? Why do so many of us look and act weighted down? Why do too many of us feel tired before, during, and after our daily work? Why are we so listless at home that our spouses and children take notice and mention it to us?

There are many right answers. More careful attention to exercise, diet, and schedule can greatly ease the burden of many ministers. But I think there is something deeper to consider. I am speaking about genuinely accepting and celebrating God's grace, deeply and personally. If the joy of the Lord is our strength, as Scripture suggests, that joy must find a dwelling place inside of us.

Third, when we start ministry positioned to receive from God, our glad acceptance dispenses freedom to our ministries. God's love is unconditional—no strings attached. Divine love refuses to demand certain actions from its recipients. Receiving God's magnanimous love sets off a marvelous chain reaction. In accepting God's love, we are empowered in turn to give and love freely without expecting anything in return. This capacity is sorely needed amongst ministers.

> They have given so much that they finally run out of spiritual and nervous energy, and what remains is underlying resentment. You find a great deal of resentment and sourness among clergy. [They] have given more than [they] had to give, and gotten very little back.[5]

While it is understandable that ingratitude may leave its mark of stinging wounds on ministers and others employed as "givers," it is a mistake to link one's sense of worth with human expressions of gratitude. Sometimes the expressions come, and they are wonderful to receive. The point here is that we should not be dependent on expressions of gratitude. Sometimes they do not come when we want them; sometimes they do not come at all.

But there is a well of appreciation that is always available. The source of love that never runs dry is the welcoming heart of God. As we receive God's warm embrace, we are released from over-dependence on the affection of others. We are able to give without expecting anything in return.

When the Pebble Hits the Rock

It is one thing to talk about sacred silence; it is another thing to arrive there spiritually. In our world that is characterized by so much doing, sacred silence is next to impossible. Yet the same thing can be said of silence as was said of jazz music one evening by Pulitzer Prize-winning composer and trumpeter Wynton Marsalis: "If we are ready to listen, it is there to be heard." If we are willing to spend time listening, holy silence may be observed, even amid the amplified volume of contemporary living.

In his book *Your Sacred Self*, Wayne Dyer offers what I believe is a wonderful metaphor and method for coming to sacred silence. He suggests that we image the transitions in consciousness, which may take place during times of prayer and meditation, as a pebble dropping through the depths of a pond. As you begin the journey toward stillness, imagine the pebble hitting the surface of the pond as the place where anxious thoughts dart about in your mental pool like minnows. This is where most of us can begin our time of quieting down. Dyer defines the next stage of calming as the pebble dropping to a second layer of the pond, the place where thinking is slowed to a point where our reflection, although still rapid, is tempered by analysis. Here the pebble is in the space where we question some of the substance of our reflection. According to Dyer, at this level, "You may catch yourself analyzing something and make an effort to stop, but at this level there is a continual movement of analyzing."[6]

The pebble in Dyer's metaphor continues dropping to the next level of the pond, a place where there is a distinct awareness of diminished chatter and analysis. At this point silence begins to set in. If we are patient and relentless in our pursuit of silence, the pebble moves through two more depths—level four, which Dyer characterizes as stillness and bliss, and level five:

> This is the final resting place deep within the mind. This is beyond quieting the mind. Here is the place within, where you empty your mind of all thoughts and experience the still point. You are unified with God and the energy of love that is at the center of all.[7]

I link Dyer's metaphor and method to the magnificent promise in Isaiah

26:3-4: "Those of steadfast mind you keep in peace—in peace because they trust in you. Trust in the Lord forever, for in God you have an everlasting rock." The silence we long for so much and neglect so often is the peace of God—*the holiness that holds us, and that is ours to hold, when the pebble hits the rock.*

No Sitting—No Soaring

I had been in the hotel room only a few minutes when I noticed the two paintings of birds on the wall. I could tell that the same person probably painted them both. When I looked at the artist's signature, I was right. Not only did they have a common artist, but the paintings also shared common features—bright, colorful, with birds perched on tree limbs. Questions then began popping into my head. Is this the same bird in both pictures? More thorough observation revealed that they were not identical. Are the environments the same? Although there were common indicators, it appeared that one painting had more of a winter quality to it. And then I wondered: Have the birds just landed, or are they perched in preparation to fly? After careful observation, including looking for either fatigue or anticipation in the eyes of the birds, I concluded that I couldn't be sure one way or the other.

But in the unknowing of the moment, another knowing settled into my consciousness, unannounced and uninvited: Whether having flown or preparing to fly, if the birds flew without ceasing, eventually they would fall to the earth in fatal exhaustion. *No sitting—no soaring.*

We are like birds. Although we are made to fly and reach for the stars of exploration, discovery, and achievement, we are not designed to fly without ceasing. Indeed, we cannot soar without periods of sitting and stopping, and the sitting is not an off-the-cuff, tangential matter. Furthermore, I do not think that sitting is something birds do grudgingly, as a quick and bothersome break from flying. It is a qualitative time of rest, refreshment, healing, play, and communication for birds, the latter of which meets human ears as singing. Perhaps for birds, sitting is no less exciting and dynamic than flying. For certain, their experiences in the heights depend on their attention to themselves in the depths.

Abraham Heschel verbalized the prerequisite power of silence, especially as it pertains to ministry:

> The strength of faith is in silence, and in words that hibernate and wait. Uttered faith must come out as surplus of silence, as the fruit of lived faith, of enduring intimacy.[8]

P.S. Your Tank Needs More Than You Think

At the gas pump one morning, the attendant surprised me by telling me that I owed him $12.00 for the sale. I was surprised because my tank was empty and I had asked him to fill it up, which usually amounted to at least $25.00. When I questioned him, he said that the price was low because he could only get that amount of gas into the tank. My curiosity was piqued even more. If my gauge was showing empty, why was he only able to pump such a limited amount of gas? He offered to try again. This time, undoubtedly much to his economic satisfaction, he was able to pump an additional $13.00 worth of gas. He found that, after all, he *could* get more fuel into the tank.

As you seek to get to the back of the boat more often, the new euphoria of *some* rest where there was none may lead you into thinking that *some* is enough. You may begin to cut back on your back-of-the-boat time. You may feel guilty for not doing as much as you feel you ought, although a great deal of our restless doing is repetitious and non-creative. Do not sell yourself short on back-of-the-boat time. Get there frequently and completely. Get there on purpose and with an attitude. Get there with deliberate delight, and without apology. Set aside time each day for devotion and play. Take momentary respites throughout the workday. Celebrate one day per week as your sabbath. Take periodic vacations, both short and extended. As you get more comfortable going to the back of the boat, your capacity for its refreshing properties will increase. You will not become lazy or lax for hanging out in the back of the boat. Rather, you will begin to live with new strength, vigor, and excitement. You will find that you need much more of rest's vital fuel than you think.

---

[1] Tilden Edwards, "Living the Day from the Heart," *Living with God in the Word*, John S. Mogabgab, ed. (Nashville: Upper Room Books, 1993), 55.

[2] Madeline L'Engle, *Glimpses of Grace* (New York: HarperCollins, 1996), 247.

[3] Anthony De Mello, *Wellsprings* (New York: Doubleday, 1985), 12.

[4] Quoted in A. W. Tozer, *The Pursuit of God* (Camp Hill, Pa.: Christian Publications, 1995), 47.

[5] Thomas Maeder, "Wounded Healers," *The Atlantic Monthly*, January, 1989, 42.

[6] Wayne Dyer, *Your Sacred Self* (New York: HarperCollins, 1995), 161.

[7] Ibid., 164.

[8] Abraham Heschel, *Moral Grandeur and Spiritual Audacity*, Susannah Heschel, ed. (New York: Noonday Press, 1996), 264.

CHAPTER NINE

The Blessings of the Back of the Boat

Throughout our educational pursuits, we enroll in courses that are required and others that are electives. The rationale is that basic courses supply fundamental knowledge that, among other things, may enhance one's educational experience in the elective courses. The back of the boat should not be seen as an elective. By so doing, we minimize the importance of respite and play, to our own detriment. But we need not embrace the necessity of rest mournfully, as if too much of life is missed by breaking away from its demands. An example of this can be seen in younger children. Although they resist going to bed, rest is the key to their wide eyes and fiery energy the next morning. The fact is, the back of the boat is not backing away from life but experiencing essential dimensions of life that we all too frequently ignore. The back of the boat holds a variety of wonderful blessings for us, if we only are willing to accept them.

Welcoming You Home

Before God calls us to *do,* God calls us to *be*. Before God calls us to be *ministers,* God calls us to be *persons.*

One of the tragedies of vocational ministry is that many of us lose ourselves in the process of becoming professional ecclesiastical servants. It happens innocently and slowly. We begin with a burning passion inside to do good, to help people, and to make the world a better place by trying to console or remove some of life's hurts. As we learn more and more about the nature of our good works, we are encouraged to greater proficiency via education and experience. Before we know it, we are asked to do more and more tasks by more and more people. Initially, the feeling of being needed is a source of great satisfaction, but then a cloud begins to settle over our sacred competency. It is a phenomenon I call "the curse of the competent." When we continue to accept these increasing demands, we are no longer ourselves; we are our work. We are no longer persons; we are what we do. The downward spiral begins. The work loses its luster; the requests of people begin to feel like pinches on our skin. Resentment builds up inside; the body becomes tired; important relationships become strained. We begin to wonder why and how our dream turned to a nightmare—and we want out.

One of the blessings of the back of the boat, which is perhaps the best blessing of all, is that we have time to rediscover ourselves away from the trappings of our vocation. And, who we are is wonderful beyond measure. Of all the persons who have lived, or who ever will live, not a one of them will be like you. The "you" to whom I am referring is not just the professional you, but the emotional, physical, and spiritual you who has life and value apart from your vocational calling. This you is too precious to lose in the stormy sea of overload and hurry. This you is too precious to lose, period.

Charles Johnson has written a provocative novel entitled *Dreamer.* It is the story of Chaym Smith, a fictional character whose striking physical resemblance to Martin Luther King Jr. earns him the job as stand-in for King. But although Smith looks like King, he is not King. When we allow what we do to ramble roughshod over who we are, we may bear a physical resemblance to ourselves, but we are not our real selves. And after a while, we don't even look like ourselves anymore.

On my desk at home is a picture of me at age six or seven. My eyes are clear and wide, and my huge ears flank my smile, which is full of interest and anticipation. I keep that picture nearby as a reminder of the me that was me, minus the robe of professional responsibility. Moreover, this child-me is still me, keeping alive my thirst for play and fun, wandering and wondering. This me has doubts and fears, but one thing is sure: He is glad to be alive. When this me, the soul-me, is nurtured and allowed to live, I am blessed beyond measure and feel like *I am*. And it is in this magnificent overflow that work may be experienced as more delight than drudgery. Persons who are awake, aware, and alive tend to make better laborers in general and ministers in particular.

Annie Dillard tells of a dream she had at a time in her life when she was learning, with limited success, how to split wood:

> One night, while all this had been going on, I had a dream in which I was given to understand, by the powers that be, how to split wood. You aim, said the dream—of course!—at the chopping block. It is true you aim at the chopping block, not at the wood; then you split the wood, instead of chipping it. You cannot do the job cleanly unless you treat the wood as the transparent means to an end, by aiming past it.[1]

In a way, I am challenging you with this back-of-the-boat and savoring-pace business to aim past vocation to reach personhood. In the process, you will be a better minister or caregiver; you will split the wood, instead of chipping it.

In perhaps the best-known verse in the Bible, John 3:16, we are told that God wishes that we live and, through it all, that we not perish. Usually we limit the application of that text to spiritual perishing *after* death. *I do not think that it is God's will that we perish* before *death either.*

A More Pleasant Spouse

Most caregivers, and clergy in particular, naturally hide our resentments and our hostilities in the company of those to whom we minister. We do not want people to think badly of us or to use their glimpse at a different side of our humanity to harm our ministry. But there are persons who are not shielded from the sides of us that are short, impatient, rude, and at times, even violent. Those persons are our spouses. Clergy's spouses are, in too many marriages, the dumping ground for the deep-seated anger that we clergy hold inside of us; the same is often true for the partners of all caregivers. Sometimes, and maybe more often than not, the marital relationship is strained less by eruptions of anger, and more by the slow leaks of frustration to which we subject our spouses day after day, night after night. Perhaps even worse than the eruptions and the slow leaks is a kind of lazy indifference with which some pastors regard their spouses. The dynamic, passionate, and energetic minister of God can become, in the time it takes to drive home, a listless, lightless shell of a spouse.

Rekindling a sense of self and wellness can have the powerful result of also rekindling relationships gone sour. In part this happens because pastors who frequent the back of the boat empty ourselves, including our fears and frustrations, in the silence and solitude of communion with God. When our loving spouses are spared totally from hearing and bearing our anguish, that personal/professional anguish is not allowed to become the overriding feature of the marital relationship.

Back-of-the-boat relinquishment and refreshment fills and frees us to be more pleasant, attentive, and festive spouses. We become easier persons to be around. Inasmuch as we disrobe our ministerial roles and expectations during times of respite and play, more time spent in the back of the boat helps us to be increasingly more comfortable being "out of ministry" with our spouses. How many times are we dining with our spouses physically, but thinking about professional obligations mentally? How many times are we late for commitments with our spouses, or end up cutting time with them short because of overloaded ministerial schedules? How often do our workloads preclude us from scheduling quality time with our spouses?

This has been particularly true of clergy*men*. Many male pastors can stand to become better husbands. However, for men and women both, a call to ministry is not a recall from the commitment of love and time required in a marriage relationship. Get to the back of boat more often, and ask your spouse to join you from time to time. Your marriage will become the passionate, deepening relationship that you both deserve, and that God encourages. Fanning the fire of ministry does not mean dousing the flame of marriage.

A More Present Parent

Nelson Mandela has told the story of one of his children saying to him, "Though you are the father of our nation, you have never had the time to be my father." As you might imagine, former President Mandela was deeply hurt by the reality of the remark. Most of us will never, ever bear the awesome responsibilities shouldered by Mandela, yet we risk our children saying something similar one day.

Several years ago, for a doctoral research project, I interviewed the daughter of a late legendary pastor. The interview, held in her father's old study, began when this accomplished, middle-aged woman blurted out, "I hate this church!"

Stunned by her confession, I asked, "Why do you say that?"

She responded without hesitation, "I hate this church because they took my daddy from me." She went on, "And sometimes I hate my father because he let them do it."

Churches, more unknowingly than purposely, can cause children to become emotional orphans. And unconsciously, but no less painfully, pastors can allow ourselves to be taken away from our children. A call to a congregation is not a call away from our children. It is our responsibility to realize that and to make others realize it, too.

Practically, this means that you may want to include a weekly family day, as well as sabbath day, in your contract. This means that you will have two days off from the church. If that sounds generous, remember that most employees have two days off from work, usually Saturdays and Sundays. Limit the number of evenings that you are away from home to one or two nights a week. Use the flexibility of the pastor's schedule to attend weekly school functions, which many 9-to-5 working parents wish they could leave work to attend. There are countless other ways that you can ensure that your children do not get the crumbs of your attention and energy.

Our youngest daughter, Jovonna, once asked me two questions that I have never forgotten: "Daddy, why do you look so sad all the time?" I was taken aback. My immediate response was "Baby, I'm not sad; I'm thinking." She said, "Yeah, well, why are you always thinking?"

I was convicted by my then five-year-old child's observation. I realized that a great many times when I was home, presumably away from work, that work was not away from me. It was so visible that "Jo-Jo" had picked it up and, in her own way, called me on it. Ever since that time I have endeavored always to be fully present with my children when I am with them.

I consider my solitary back-of-the-boat time helpful to ensuring that the person my children see is not a pastor first, but a loving father who is focused exclusively on them for some precious moments during the day. When I am together with Jasmine, Jared, Joya, and Jovonna, especially in silly frolic, it is wonderful back-of-the-boat group experience. One of the things I have done over the years is to make up and sing crazy songs. Some of the best times of all for me are singing these wild songs in succession with my kids. Friday night, our family night, is a time to play games, see movies, or just be together. We fuss, we fight, we laugh, we play, but most important, we are with one another.

Of all the honors I have received, none is more meaningful to me than a letter written by my then eleven-year-old son. I am committed to living in and up to his words. He concluded the paper that he had written about me for a school project with the following paragraph:

> Now, you're probably saying he is very, very busy. How much time does he have for his family? Well the answer is lots. He always has time for me and my sisters, and my mother. He also has time to play his computer games, drive us places, and buy us things. It is an honor for me to have him as my dad.

I'll take that accolade over a Pulitzer Prize any day!

Healthier Congregations

One of the best things that a pastor can give a congregation is responsibility for ministry. I do not believe that Jesus ever intended for so much of ministry to fall into the hands of a few "ordained" persons, leaving congregations dependent because they perceive ordination as a prerequisite for ministry. Congregations are severely handicapped by such dependencies. Local churches being referred to, not by the name of the church, but by the pastor's name is one of the clearest manifestations of this widespread drawback. We speak of Reverend Johnson's church or Pastor Smith's congregation. How sad it is that ministerial functions, including counseling, teaching, and leading, are domesticated into the hands of a few "called" individuals who rarely realize that their ministerial monopoly keeps others from assuming appropriate church and community responsibilities.

The hidden but widespread ecclesiastical ineptitude of the masses is revealed for all to see in the wake of a "great" pastor's death—when that person's "great" ministry flounders and dies. Truly great pastors know that the ministers of the church are the people of the church. Truly great pastors do not need to monopolize ministry out of ego gratification, or any other negative factor influencing to ministry performance. Truly great pastors know that getting out of the way is an integral action in leadership empowerment. Moreover, truly great pastors know that modeling self-care and family attentiveness can contribute immeasurably to positive church spirit and morale. Therefore, back-of-the-boat time is not just a strategy for personal well being, but also a strategy for encouraging more effective congregational life and mission.

Charged Creativity

When the disciples awakened Jesus at the height of the storm's rage, they were like alarmed children alerting a parent to trouble. What do you suppose they thought Jesus would do? Did they think he would pray with them and calm their fearful hearts? Did they think that his mere presence with them out on the deck would make the situation more bearable in some way? Was their rushing to Jesus a sort of knee-jerk reaction to the threatening winds and waves? They probably did not expect Jesus to do anything; they just couldn't keep still. Whatever the disciples expected that night, the result of their petition was beyond their wildest imaginings.

After attending to the alarming cries of his disciples, Jesus turned his attention to the storm. The disciples barely could see each other and Jesus due to the storm, which in the pre-meteorological age was thought by some to be caused by evil spirits. But they heard Jesus speak—not to them, but to the storm itself. And in a moment that the disciples would remember for the rest of their lives, the storm ceased—instantaneously—in uncanny obedience to Jesus' command. As one storm ended, however, another one commenced: The disciples were filled with questions and fears about the nature of Jesus' humanity and the magnitude of his power, which appeared to be without limits.

There were many ways to approach the crisis that night, but Jesus' way was nontraditional, to say the least. His approach to the storm that night was not only a testimony to his divinity, but also to his human creativity. What a daring, innovative solution! Who else on the boat that night would have thought to talk back to the storm? Jesus' response is not only an example of what *God* can do, but of what *people* can do when inspired and empowered by God.

Rest—or backing away from engagement—is a tremendous channel of creativity, "the process of bringing something new into being."[2] Could it be that Jesus was able to approach the ferocious storm in a new way, in large part, because he had taken the time to refresh himself in the back of the boat?

Linda Schierse Leonard makes the point afresh in her stimulating work *The Call to Create*:

> A major obstacle to creativity is wanting to be in the peak season of growth and generation at all times. For example, if we want to be productive all of the time, we may push ourselves beyond our natural limits and not acknowledge our bodily and psychological needs for rest and regeneration. This is an unrealistic expectation because the creative process has necessary ebbs and flows like those of nature.[3]

We live in a time of great challenge. Our capacity to think in new ways and develop new paradigms and ways of communicating has never been more crucial. Proper respite is essential to nurturing genuine creativity. It was no accident that one of Jesus' most extraordinary actions occurred immediately after he had taken time to rest, to inhale. There is an inextricable link between back-of-the-boat respite and bow-of-the-boat activism. Tilden Edwards words it well:

> Contemplation and action are not independent realms. They are meant to be intimately connected, as we see in Jesus' life and in the heart of Judeo-Christian tradition, but in practice they are often insulated from each other.[4]

Ellen J. Langer makes a case for charged creativity, not just as a dynamic momentary interlude, but also as a way life. For Langer, creativity hinges on mindfulness, a quality which evidences three characteristics: (1) creation of new categories; (2) openness to new information; and (3) awareness of more than one perspective. Mindfulness, according to Langer, is the direct opposite of mindlessness in which we are trapped by categories, practice uncritical thinking, and act from a single perspective.[5] I understand Langer's argument to be an expansion of that perennial plea we hear from good parents and teachers early in life: Pay attention! Langer suggests that we pay *wide* attention, in ways that allow for broad learning and far-reaching visioning and accomplishment.

I could not agree more with Langer's encouragement of a sustained life of thinking and doing "outside the box" in new ways and toward new ends. To me, this rings true to the spirit of our faith, which is about "making all things new." Yet we must understand that regular such adventures of the spirit and mind need constant nourishment. Sustained creativity requires regular rest; dynamic mindfulness springs forth from the ground of determined silence.

In his book *Sabbath*, Wayne Muller argues that rest is not only essential to meeting the huge challenge of crises, it is essential to satisfying the demands of proficient problem-solving on a daily basis. If we do not take time to go to the back of the boat, more often than not we end up, as Muller puts it, "Doing good badly." [6]

Restored Vocational Joy

I have come across two book passages to which I have returned many times and which I have discussed in a variety of settings. In the first passage, writer Donald Hall describes the onset of "the best day":

> The best day begins with waking early—I check the clock: Damn! It's only 3:00 A.M.—because I want so much to get out of bed and start working. Usually something particularly beckons so joyously—like a poem that I have good hope for, that seems to go well. Will it look as happy today as it looked yesterday? By four-thirty I can wait no longer. . . . I feel work-excitement building, joy-pressure mounting—until I need resist it no more but sit at the desk and open the folder that holds the day's beginning, its desires and its hope.[7]

The second passage is a selection from Lewis Porter's critically acclaimed biography on the great jazz artist John Coltrane:

> Right by Coltrane's apartment was a private after-hours (early morning) place, the Woodbine Club, at Twelfth and Master, where local musicians would jam on weekends. Mary Alexander says that such artists as Lester Young, Coleman Hawkins, and Duke Ellington would show up there after gigs elsewhere in town. Saxophonist and composer Benny Golson, born January 25, 1929, exclaims: "Oh, it was so fertile, man! Every day was an adventure. We wanted to sleep fast so we could wake up and [start again].[8]

These two accounts are most fascinating to me because they speak of work-joy. For too many persons, including too many pastors, labor has become a mild form of slavery—and some would not include the descriptive modifier. We spend far too much time doing the work of our vocation to be bored to death by it until we die. The lyrics of a popular song of the black church sound forth: "This joy I have, the world didn't give it to me. . . . The world didn't give it, the world can't take it away."[9] That may be true in terms of how we feel about our salvation, but it is sadly untrue for many when it comes to the matters of vocation.

How many of us pastors wake up with the excitement for work burning inside of us, as in the case of Donald Hall? How many of us go to bed longing for the moment when our feet will strike ground in pursuit of another day's adventures? How many of us remain filled with joy for the work of ministry? The sad, undeniable truth is that too many pastors have had the joy of ministry sucked out of us by overload and hurry. The ensuing plea of an overloaded minister's prayer may not be David's words in Psalm 51 exactly, but the urgency is the same: "Lord, restore unto me the joy of my vocation."

The back of the boat boosts vocational joy in a deeply spiritual way. Taking time away from it all provides precious time for reflecting on the fundamental *meaning* of it all—that we are the beloved of God, called by God to live and laugh, to give and grow. There are countless ways to live out God's dream, but as we discover those manifold ways, we must not forget that life is God's great and wondrous gift to us. The back of the boat gives us the opportunity to picture our problems and challenges against the backdrop of divine love and calling.

The back of the boat is a place to celebrate the "God-ness" and goodness of life once again. This is a way for us to get into God, and for God to get into us. The inevitable result is more joy and enthusiasm for life in general, and for vocation in particular. And enthusiasm is precisely the right word to use here. Our word "enthusiasm" is derived from the Greek *enthousiazein,* which means to be inspired by a god. Enthusiasm literally means "in (*en*) God (*theos*)."

Vocational joy is restored in the back of the boat in other ways. For example, while ordinarily, reflecting on one's work should be excluded from moments of respite, there is one important exception—when we are gratefully reflecting on a ministerial high point or success. Generally, we spend far more time with our pains and our pursuits than we do with our gains and our prizes. Perhaps we would experience more joy in our work if we took more time to savor the progresses, the breakthroughs, and the miracles wrought through our own grit, determination, and no small amount of God's grace.

Another way for vocational joy to find you in the back of the boat is by using some respite time to dream outside the box—mentally resisting negative limitations you place on yourself, and which others place on you—about where you and God will be sailing next. I believe that we may be inspired to think about our vocations during leisurely moments in ways that can enhance our overall sense of appreciation for our vocation.

Power for Ministry

After nearly thirty years of preaching and nearly twenty years of pastoral/teaching ministry, I am convinced of this one thing: The deepest strength for ministry lies beyond professional and educational competencies. I do not mean to diminish such learned skills and acquired knowledge; learning is a way of loving God. To paraphrase the sentiment of the 1960s ballad "If I had a Hammer," if I had a hammer I would pound out the words, "Learn, Pastors, learn." But there are other things I would hammer. I would hammer out that soulful, life-changing ministry happens through our ability to mediate God's loving presence and power. It is not just a matter of knowing about God; it is a matter of knowing God.

The only way to mediate God is to get in the way of God, and that comes through learning and through daring to love God. God has willed that divine light come to us through persons and situations. During a mid-program review of our Master of Divinity students at Andover Newton Theological School in Newton Centre, Massachusetts, one student was given the highest compliment that any minister, student, or veteran, can receive: "She is one through whom the Spirit blows." Are we willing to let the Spirit blow through us? To let God manifest godliness through us? The prospect is a fiercely presumptuous one, but such is the foolish potency of the gospel.

With learning there must be a consuming passion and a burning thirst for God. Nothing less will satisfy the deepest calling of ministry, which is to satisfy the cavernous longing of the human soul. We cannot serve God apart from God; the power is in the Presence. It is a Presence that may be embraced anew in the dynamic solitude of the back of the boat. John Westerhoff's words find confirmation in my lengthy tenure of preaching/teaching service:

> Preachers and teachers whose lives are centered in prayer, that is, whose relationship with God comes first, will always communicate the gospel, because they have been enabled to reveal in their personal lives its attractiveness and transforming power.[10]

---

[1] Annie Dillard, *The Writing Life* (New York: Harper and Row, 1989), 43.

[2] Rollo May, *The Courage to Create* (New York: W. W. Norton, 1975), 39.

[3] Linda Schierse Leonard, *The Call to Create* (New York: Harmony Books, 2000), 7.

[4] Tilden Edwards, "Jesus and Buddha: Good Friends," *Shalem News*, Winter, 2000, 2.

[5] Ellen Langer, *Mindfulness* (Reading, Mass.: Perseus Books, 1989), 62-63.

[6] Wayne Muller, *Sabbath* (New York: Bantam Books, 1999), 157.

[7] Donald Hall, *Life Work* (Boston: Beacon Press, 1993), 41.

[8] Lewis Porter, *John Coltrane* (Ann Arbor, Mich.: University of Michigan Press, 1998), 36.

[9] "This Joy I Have," author unknown. Negro spiritual in the public domain.

[10] John Westerhoff, *Spiritual Life: The Foundation for Preaching and Teaching* (Louisville, Ky.: Westminster John Knox Press, 1994), 76.

CHAPTER TEN

Four Critical Questions

How Do I Balance Getting to the Back of the Boat with Getting the Job Done?

More than a few people will read this book and other publications like it and feel compelled to change. They will plan their transformation, but after a few valiant efforts, they will end up right back at square one. One of the reasons for the return to business as usual, after having made the commitment to change, is the business itself. Specifically, it is the need to get important things done, even at the expense of rest and play. We placate ourselves by thinking that once the work crunch subsides, we will have more time for fun. The only problem is that crunch-time rarely ends in our culture, and often our work overload is halted involuntarily by sickness rather than by choice.

I think that the balance between bow-of-the-boat activism and back-of-the-boat respite is achieved fundamentally through thinking differently. If we can win the battle in our heads, new behavior can commence and proceed. There are several key beliefs that we must embrace if we are to achieve appropriately balanced living. Fully embracing these beliefs may take a while, as they go against the grain of conventional beliefs that we have been taught, but never really challenged until now. These beliefs likely have been entrenched in our consciousness for a number of years. We also may have a certain loyalty to these old beliefs because they have played a role in nurturing the successes and achievements we have experienced in life. Changing our thinking is hard to do, yet therein lies the key to back-of-the-boat respite, liberation, and empowerment.

What are some of the fundamental beliefs that undergird a balance between respite and labor? One belief is that *personhood is as much about being as it is about doing.* This is a major revelation for persons whose sense of worth has been inextricably bound to performance, beginning with those early years when esteem was linked with pleasing parents or other loved ones. One of the greatest days of our lives is the day we first feel a joyous sensation about who we are simply *because* we are.

One way to appreciate this sensation is to reflect on what God sees, first and foremost, when God sees you, and what brings God joy, first and foremost, when God sees you. Do you perceive God as first noticing your achievements and successes? Do you sense personal achievement as being the root of God's rejoicing in you? Or can you imagine God being excited about you, just as a parent is excited about a child simply because the child exists? If you can fathom worthiness apart from works in the mind of God, chances are you will be able to do it better in your own mind. Once we get a sense of our *being-worth* having priority over our *doing-worth,* we free ourselves mentally and emotionally to pay as much or more attention to who we are as we do to what we achieve.

A second belief shift that promotes sustained change toward balanced living is understanding *the essential relationship between back-of-the-boat rest and play and the qualities of creativity, productivity, and longevity.* Take a moment and think of persons you have known who put work before anything else. Now think of their accomplishments. Then consider their family situations. Finally, consider their overall well being, if they are still alive.

People who run, run, run and work, work, work are not the most productive and creative persons in our society. In fact, a great deal of their doing actually entails repeating tasks that were not done properly the first time because of haste and lack of clarity. Moreover, the case can be made that overload and hurry are great social liabilities. Consider the hidden social and financial costs to society due to family neglect and abuse, stress, and related medical conditions. What about the cumulative, creative, and contributory loss to society resulting from the premature deaths of overloaded human beings—persons in their forties and fifties who died still having much uncelebrated and unshared? When these unspoken truths are identified, one thing becomes strikingly clear: We all suffer from the fatal delusion that unrestricted doing serves our best interests, both personally and collectively.

Increasing evidence affirms that respite is essential, not only for production but for higher levels of creativity. An example of this can be found in the late great poet Denise Levertov's identification of "the prime necessity" of her craft:

> The most important factor (along with native ability, of course) in any poet's survival and development is that he or she recognizes the necessity of apparently doing nothing and of giving each potential poem time to incubate. Too many would-be poets expend their energies in an effort which results in banalities, who should be letting the unknown poem work within them.[1]

How Do I Slow Down?

It is one thing to be told that you need to slow down and relax more, and moreover, to know that you need to do so. It is another thing to actually do it. The reasons why this is true are legion, including varied personal and cultural expectations and addictions. If, as was true in my case, you have grown up in the overload lane and feel that much of your success is due to your ambitious drive, it may be harder to change, even though your loved ones and the voice within may be urging you. How do you change?

First, you must engage and keep engaging in the battle of beliefs. Remember the man at the pool of Bethesda in Scripture. He had been sick for many years, and his attempts at healing had been thwarted by the people who made it to the healing waters ahead of him. This man linked his illness to the selfishness of others. The first thing Jesus did was to enter the landscape of his mind by asking him, "Do you want to be healed?" Jesus knew that how human beings think has a great deal to do with how we live, and that our *perceptions* govern our *receptions.* When it comes to personal growth, we can only receive what we allow ourselves to perceive. In the case of the man at the pool, Jesus linked internal perception to external condition. What the man thought about his condition was a factor in improving his condition.

Unloading and slowing down involve a change of mind and heart about fundamental beliefs regarding God, personhood, work, play, and rest. Review some of the passages in this book that address these matters and bounce them off of your beliefs. What you believe has the power to liberate you or to incarcerate you. For instance, if you believe that God is pleased most of all by your work and service, chances are you will be striving constantly to do more and more. This belief will fuel your conscious and unconscious behavior. But if you believe that God values your creative pursuits and is *equally* pleased that you are living and enjoying blessings—including the blessings of spending time with family, friends, and self—you are less likely to drown in the waters of vocational overload. In both cases, what you believe is the critical factor. Your beliefs can give you forward momentum, or they can keep you stuck in the mud.

A similar case can be made for your views on play. You may believe play to be the domain of children and irresponsible adults who do not take life as seriously as they should. Such underdeveloped notions of play can lead to a complete negation of play-related qualities, including spontaneity, risk, and joy. On the other hand, if you can fathom play as a continuing holy reality that is just as valuable to adults as it is to children, then you are less likely to discount its value in your life as both a person and minister. If you value the role of play for adults, you will find it easier to schedule play, and to revel in it without guilt when it interrupts your daily schedule. Play, in the latter mindset, is legitimized by the sheer delight it offers.

Another important belief that you may need to overhaul is your belief about change. Even though ministers preach conversion and transformation, when we get beyond spiritual change, we are as resistant to change as anyone. Making behavioral changes is as threatening to ministers as it is to everyone else. Many of us resist change out of fear; others shy away from change because we have made ourselves comfortable in our current state. Others see change as a confession of shortcoming or failure, as a backing-down from a set course, as an admission that we are insufficient and inadequate. For still others, a negative estimation of change may be rooted in a procession of bad transitional experiences; thus, change has come to represent something ominous and oppressive.

Of course, there is another way to view change. Change can be seen as an avenue to something new and better. I believe that some folks rightfully interpret change as a basic and essential rhythm of life. Inspirational speaker Loretta LaRoche has said, "We ought to regularly be doing something that remakes us."[2] This kind of attitude about change can open a person to new vistas about life, including matters of vocational fulfillment and balance.

As you consider and reconsider your fundamental beliefs, be prepared to invent new practices. I am convinced of this one thing: You will not overcome overload doing the things the way you are now. You will have to make changes—some big ones—in the way you lead your life. For me, overcoming has meant making significant changes, including waking up early to do the things that I love, setting aside midmorning hours for study and preparation, limiting evenings away from home to two a week, and celebrating a weekly sabbath.

And then there were the "big small" changes, including reviewing a savoring pace meditation once a day, reading poetry, listening to jazz often as I work, and allowing for more margin (or empty space) throughout the day. As you strive toward overcoming, your strategies will develop along the way, as have mine. Although there will be commonalities, no two ways of realizing a living balance between respite, play, and labor will be identical. The important thing is to embrace the vision of living wholeness, and then to live in that vision with vigilant effort.

What Do I Tell the Critics?

Some people in our hyperactive culture perceive slowing down and resisting overload as negligence. It is helpful to appreciate the varied contexts out of which these critics are operating. Some are *veterans* of overload who expect others to shoulder the excess weight in the same manner that they have done. Others are overload *victims* who feel that if they have to suffer through it, others should not be exempt from misery. Still others are persons who have learned to *accommodate* overload during periods when a great deal of work needs to be accomplished. Thus, they see overload as a necessary periodic reality of the workplace. As you dialogue with your critics—including the toughest critic of all, the one in your own mirror—try to discern whether you are talking to a veteran, a victim, or an accommodater.

The veteran may not be open to your rationale for overload resistance. As far as she is concerned, you need to be more like her. Your best witness to her will be quality work produced at a savoring pace. When that gets her attention, you may have a chance to explain yourself. But with the veteran, action will speak louder than words. In the church setting, such action may find expression in sermons that are delivered with more care and passion. Pastoral conversations will receive the whole you, rather than a piece of you. This kind of qualitative, mindful ministry is its own justification.

The victim, in time, is more open to your change of priority and pace. Possibly jealous and angry initially, at some point he will want to know how you have come to the place of vocational peace and balance. Patiently talk about your experience and encourage him to develop comparable strategies toward wholeness in living. The victim in the congregation may be that person who initially is outraged because you have not seen more of the sick and shut-in members. In time, this person may be led to confess his own bondage to unrealistic expectations. Until then, know that some of the negative energy directed at you is, in part, his personal disgust at being locked in the inextricable grip of overload.

The accommodater critic may be the most difficult of all. Such persons will acknowledge appreciation for drawing back, but only after the work is done. This critic may be the one that most ministers emulate. We are good at giving our all in "crunch time" and telling ourselves, "I'll get a break when we get through the challenge." The challenge may be a building project, a series of religious services, or a family crisis that demands ongoing counseling.

Real problems exist within the accommodater perspective. First, it suggests that there are no costs associated with pushing ourselves to the limit, as long as there is some period of rest, albeit brief, after the crunch. What accommodaters forget is the cumulative stress that is built up by chronic crunch times. Simply taking a couple of days off at the end of the push cannot relieve the damage done by constantly going to the wire. The head and heart remember the strain. Second, the accommodater perspective suggests that the body is always in a state of readiness to undertake intensive work for prolonged periods of time. This is not the case. Often we undertake demanding projects in weakened physical, emotional, and physical states. Our adrenaline carries us, but damage is being done. Third, the accommodater perspective presumes that it is all right to place valuable persons, namely self, spouse, children, and friends, on hold until the work is done.

While we cannot avoid completely those necessary periods of extravocational sacrifice, we must resist an ethic that condones such sacrifice as a way of life. This is work idolatry. All idolatry, no matter how laudable, is unholy. The answer to the accommodater critic (including the one in the mirror) is this: Sustained vocational balance is better, in both the short and long term, than revolving intervals of overload and pseudo rest. Our souls and loved ones are to be cared for daily through established rhythms of mutually nourishing rest, play, and labor. Long stretches of personal and familial abuse cannot be justified, neither on the grounds of obligation nor theology.

How Do I Know If I Am Doing Too Much?

There are many signals that indicate overdoing. One of the great problems is that it is hard to hear the signals while we are ensnared by overload. At those times, we simply are carrying too much and going too fast to notice. But the signals are there and paying more than a moment's notice to a few of them can set us on the road of positive transformation.

In his book *Overdoing It: How to Slow Down and Take Care of Yourself*, Bryan Robinson described three progressive stages of work addiction. I have summarized and charted his findings below:

Early Stage

- rushing, busyness
- inability to say no
- constantly thinking of work
- overvaluation of one's own ability
- no days off

Middle Stage

- regularly working more than forty hours per week
- onset of other addictions, including addictions to food and alcohol, relationships, money, etc.
- chronic fatigue
- aborted attempts to slow down and do less

Late Stage

- physical pain
- emotional deadness
- moral and spiritual bankruptcy

In my own experience, I have become keenly aware of the early signs that I am doing too much. I believe that early awareness is essential to avoiding the waters of overload altogether. Here are twelve of my early warning signals:

1. Going more than one day without spending time in the back of the boat
2. Losing my sense of humor for more than a day
3. Missing a basic gratitude for life for more than a day
4. Not having a moment when my spouse or children request one, and putting stringent time limits on it when I do have a moment
5. Missing unhurried quality time with my wife and children
6. Feeling resentful toward others about "all I have to do"
7. Being intolerant and unappreciative of the unscheduled surprises and silences offered in any given day
8. Having our youngest daughter ask me, "Why do you look so sad?"

9. Rushing my listening and speaking in conversations
10. Exhibiting inflexibility when I am forced to alter my schedule
11. Going to bed late too many consecutive nights
12. Mindlessly "getting through" a day

You will identify your own signals that alert you to the fact that you may be doing too much. Take a moment to note them. Now, do something else: Promise your family that from this day forward, you will pay more attention to them. The quality of your life and of your vocation depends on it.

---

[1] Denise Levertov, "The Prime Necessity," *The Writer's Chronicle*, October-November, 1999, 43.

[2] Loretta LaRoche, in a speech given at Bay Path College, Long Meadow, Maryland. Winter 1999.

CHAPTER ELEVEN

The One Thing That Is Everything

Luke 10:38-42

The Tension Mounts

As I read this biblical story, I can't help thinking that Martha wishes she had performed the chore assigned to Mary. Maybe the sisters had drawn up a list of duties for each of them to complete related to hosting their friend Jesus. One of Mary's tasks may have been to wash Jesus' feet. This was a customary act of kindness extended to guests by their hosts, guests who likely had walked many miles down Palestine's dry and dusty roads of sand. Guests looked forward to this cleansing and soothing act of hospitality before dining.

I imagine the sisters had agreed that Mary would perform this task on their honored guest. But based on the text, I believe that Martha had begun to wish she had done it, because Mary had washed Jesus' feet all right, and that was all that she had done. In fact, she had taken a court-side seat at his feet! The used towel and the bowl of water had been pushed aside, and she was locked in conversation with Jesus, mostly listening to him.

As the scenario unfolds, I imagine that at first Martha is not paying much attention to Mary and Jesus as she is caught up in the busyness of her own tasks. Eventually, she realizes that she is the only one working. She tries to get Mary's attention. At first, she probably gives Mary some "get a move on" glances, but to no avail. Next, she brushes up against Mary in passing, holding several dishes; but still no response. Anger begins to well up inside of her, and Martha whispers hard in her sister's ear, "We've got work to do!" No response.

Finally, Martha has enough. She cannot get Mary to pay attention to her, so she decides to interrupt Jesus. "Er, excuse me, Jesus," she breaks in, "I sure could use some help in getting *somebody* to do some work around here, Lord." Reading between the lines, I understand that Martha is not only sending a message to Mary; she is sending a message to Jesus. "Jesus, if you want to eat, you had better finish whatever it is you are saying to my sister, quick and in a hurry. In fact, if you want to say something to her, tell her to get to work!"

Perhaps Jesus is jarred a bit by Martha's abruptness because he is equally engaged and delighted by the dialogue as Mary. Nonetheless, he recovers and says, not to Mary but to the sister in distress, "Martha, you have a lot on your mind, maybe too much. There is really one essential thing with which you need to be concerned. And at this point, I think your sister understands that better than you do."

This is where the scene fades to black and the tape runs out. We are left to imagine what happened next. I can imagine three distinct but equally compelling scenarios.

The Confrontation

In the first imaginary conclusion, Martha is put off by Jesus' response; in fact, Jesus touches her last nerve! "How dare you take her side?" she demands to know. I see her looking first at Mary, and then at Jesus. She then shoves the tray into Jesus' hands saying, "If that's the way you feel about it, here's the one thing you'll need to do: You and Mary can get your own food. I quit!"

In the second possible ending, I see Mary hearing Martha and really seeing her sister for the first time since Jesus arrived. She realizes what a poor hostess she has been. Realizing that Martha has been doing all of the work, I see Mary getting up and taking the tray from her sister in one sweeping motion. I hear her saying, "Martha, I am sorry that I haven't been more help to you. I guess I got caught up in what Jesus was saying. Jesus, please forgive me. Can we finish our talk later?" Jesus nods and smiles as the two sisters walk off together.

In the final fabricated scenario, Martha hears Jesus' response and she is stunned by it. It is not so much that Jesus has taken sides; rather, something he said has gone directly inside her and taken up residence. She pauses a moment, and without responding to Jesus or looking at Mary, she turns and walks slowly and mindfully back to the kitchen. She places the tray on the counter, sits down, and lets her face fall into her hands. She wonders, "What on earth did Jesus mean when he said that there's only one thing that I really need?"

Reflection and Introspection

Some time passes and, in the stillness, Martha admits there is something warmly inviting about what Jesus has said. Two words in particular resonate inside of her: "one thing." Martha knows herself to be a person of many things. She thinks about many things, and she likes doing many things; that is how she perceives and defines herself. She always busy doing something, and she enjoys it—most of the time. But there are those times—and truthfully, she has begun to have them more and more—when she longs for more joy in her doing, and even more peace. More and more, she longs for a steadier mode of thinking and doing so that she will not feel so disjointed. Her sanity is still intact, perhaps, but she is also mixed up and confused.

She thinks to herself, "Humph! Jesus isn't telling me anything that I haven't told myself already." She recognizes the wisdom in his suggestion that Mary is on to something that she would do well to heed. Martha is not disturbed simply because her sister is sitting at Jesus' feet, learning from him. Rather, she is troubled that Mary can allow herself to stop, sit, and listen at any time, regardless of the other demands on her time;

Martha wishes she possessed just a little of that quality. There are times when Martha wishes she did not feel so driven. Mary knows when and how to stop; Martha wishes she could learn.

Perhaps Martha tells herself, "People see my busyness; thank God they can't see my restlessness and my discomfort. Maybe the busyness is connected to those feelings. . . . Wait a minute! Did Jesus see my restlessness? Is the 'one thing' he referred to part of the answer I am looking for? Is it the answer?"

The Insight

The one thing that Jesus said is needed appears again and again as a fine, brilliant thread woven throughout Scripture. Four texts may be used as a caption under a photograph of Mary at the feet of Jesus, the lasting portrait of the one thing who is everything:

> Be still, and know that I am God. (Psalm 46:10, NIV)

> Thou will keep him in perfect peace whose mind is stayed on thee. (Isaiah 26:3, KJV)

> Now this is eternal life: that they may know you, the only true God, and Jesus Christ, whom you have sent. (John 17:3, NIV)

> I consider everything as loss compared to the surpassing value of knowing Christ Jesus my Lord. (Philippians 3:8, NIV)

The one thing that is everything is friendship with God in Christ, because it alone can satisfy our longing for love, our thirst for peace, and our hunger for joy. It is an intimate friendship that best sanctifies our doing, supplying us with meaning, purpose, and direction that are holy *and* healthy.

We do well to remember that the "one thing" that is everything is as close as our prayerful desire to experience union and friendship with God. The question each of us must ask ourselves is "How badly do I want the one thing that is everything?"

CHAPTER TWELVE

Let There Be Laughter!

Genesis 18:9-15

Sarah's Laughter

The Bible tells us that Sarah laughed to herself when she discovered she was an expectant mother. Small wonder that Sarah is not breaking out in sidesplitting, knee-slapping, laughter. Who can blame her? What the stranger says to her is so implausible and so crazy that it is ludicrous, downright funny.

The stranger says that ninety-year-old Sarah, married to one-hundred-year-old Abraham, is going to have a baby. Sarah can hardly believe her ears. No wonder she finds herself laughing. It is not that she does not want to have a baby. In fact, she had cried over her barrenness many times through the years, especially during the early years of her marriage. But, a baby? Now? She does not laugh to keep from crying; she just laughs and wonders if Abraham's dinner guest has had a little too much wine with dinner.

But as she turns away from the tent entrance and the conversation she has just overheard, whether accidentally or on purpose, she stops dead in her tracks. Somehow, the stranger who just made that crazy statement is on to her. He overhears her laughter and asks her husband Abraham about it.

Amazingly, the stranger brings God into the picture. "Say it is possible," suggests the stranger. "Is God not able to do the impossible?" Indeed, the text suggests that, at that point, God is doing the talking, rather than the stranger.

At this, Sarah, now in full view of her husband and the stranger, denies that she had laughed. There is a pause. Will the stranger back off of his claim and offer an apology? How had he heard her anyway? How could he have heard her? How could he have known? Surely he does not want to make a scene out of this, especially after having been treated so well. All of these things probably swirl around in Sarah's mind.

I imagine that more dialogue takes place, even though it is not recorded in Genesis 18. Although Sarah lies, I believe the mysterious stranger does not judge Sarah. Instead, perhaps with a twinkle in his eye and levity in his voice, he gently refutes her denial. "Oh yes. You laughed."

That is one possible version of the unfolding of the big announcement to Abraham and Sarah. The other version I have envisioned is that of Sarah and the stranger going back and forth, like children on a playground: "You laughed," says the stranger.

"Did not," Sarah retorts.

"Did too."

"Did not."

And just when it appears that Sarah will have the last word, as the stranger walks off into the distance but before he is completely out of sight, he suddenly turns and yells, "Did too!"

When Laughter Is Not Funny

Why did Sarah deny her laughter? Perhaps she realized that she was laughing as much *at* the stranger as she was laughing at what the stranger said and that did not feel good to her. It did not sit well with her. Sarah knew what it felt like to be laughed at. She herself had been mocked for years for her barrenness.

There is a kind of laughter that should not feel good to any of us. That kind is pseudo-laughter, false laugher that needs to be denied and resisted.

In its crudest form, this is laughter directed at persons—girls, women, boys, and men—because of their race or culture. Pseudo-laughter is nothing more than a form of violence. It is dehumanizing humor that seeks to trivialize people who do not fit into our mold for life, people such as homosexuals, homeless persons, and ethnic minorities.

If Sarah was recalling and retracting her laughter because she feared she was making light of God and God's representative, good for her. But perhaps that was not the case at all. Maybe Sarah denied her laughter because she had developed the habit of doing so. Maybe through the years, family and friends had accused her of not taking life seriously. Her jokes and frivolity more often than not had been perceived as silly and childish. Maybe she had been asked more times than she wanted to remember, "When are you going to grow up?" Maybe she had been miseducated into minimizing the value of her laughter.

The Value of Laughter

Throughout our adult lives, we are given the strong, if unspoken message that laughter has no place in the things of life that are really important. Grown people are not supposed to approach life and vocation with humor. Some areas of life are deemed too serious. In the movie *Patch Adams,* a young, unorthodox physician-in-training is almost dismissed from medical school, in part for displaying "excessive happiness."

Laughter and gaiety are genuine adult needs. In *The Color Purple,* a broken Sophia laments, "I know what it feels like to want to sing, and have it beat out ya." If laugher should be harnessed in everyday living, it certainly has to be restrained when it comes to religion. After all, is there anything more serious than God, anything more solemn than the holy, the sacred? Sometimes, we in the church go out of our way to ensure that people don't get too carried away. Alan Jones wrote in his wonderful book *Sacrifice and Delight*:

> In some ways the organization of the Church looks as if it has arranged things precisely to see to it that the Spirit is kept in check,

> to see that nothing happens, least of all the breaking out of delight.[1]

And, he added:

> Deadliness has a terrible mystery about it because it is not really dead. It is depressingly alive, the active enemy of delight.[2]

Maybe Sarah denied laughing because she had too many enemies of delight in her life, people who made her believe that laughter did not mix well with maturity. But Sarah had the last laugh. Nine months later, she had the laugh of her life. And that second time, she did not take it back (Genesis 21:6-7)!

Part of the fun in the miracle of Isaac's birth is that it actually happened! Ninety-year-old Sarah had a baby! Century-old Abraham became a daddy! It really happened! Can you believe it? Every time Sarah thought about it, she laughed. And she laughed even harder as she pictured the expressions on people's faces. She imagined how shocked they would be when they saw her pushing a stroller down Main Street! They would be stunned when they looked in her grocery cart and found diapers and baby powder!

Sarah was so filled with free-flowing laughter about the birth of her child—not her grandchild or great-grandchild—that she did not name the baby Abraham Jr. or any of the names that might have seemed appropriate. She named her first and only child *Isaac,* which in Hebrew means "laughter."

The stranger is not mentioned in Genesis 21:6-7, but my sense is that, unlike in Genesis 18 where Sarah was the one behind the tent curtain laughing, this time it was God behind the curtain, off-stage in the distance, laughing away.

Let There Be Laughter!

In *Martin & Malcolm & America,* James Cone notes the role of laughter in the work of the two great leaders, and the continuing power of laughter for activism today:

> To fight for life is to experience the joy of life. To laugh, to have

> fun, is to bear witness to life against death. Freedom fighters are fun-loving people. Therefore, let us laugh, let us shout for joy, not as an indication that we are no longer angry but rather as a sign that we have just begun to fight.[3]

Let there be laughter! Laughter is healing to the soul and the body, as the doctors have verified, concurring that it is one of the most potent natural stress relievers. Additionally, there are hundreds of reports verifying the value of laughter for curing illness. Some reports are nothing short of miraculous.

In *Laugh After Laugh: The Healing Power of Humor,* Dr. Raymond Moody relates the experience of a well-known clown who visited a hospital. While there, the clown noticed a little girl being fed by a nurse. Lying next to the little girl was a doll that looked like the clown. As the clown walked closer to the child, the child said his name. The nurse threw down the spoon and ran off to call the doctor. Why was the nurse so startled? That was the first time the child had spoken in six months. The child progressed daily after that breakthrough.

God Is a Clown!

Dario Fo, one of Italy's great playwrights and clowns, won the 1997 Nobel Prize for literature. When he was first informed of this, he thought it was a big joke. Assured and reassured that it was not, Fo exclaimed, "God is a clown!"

God *is* a clown. We do not find these exact words in the Scriptures, but we do find these words:

> A happy heart makes the face cheerful. (Proverbs 15:13, NIV)
> The cheerful heart has a continual feast. (Proverbs 15:15, NIV)
> Everlasting joy will crown their heads. Gladness and joy will overtake them, and sorrow and sighing will flee. (Isaiah 35:10, NIV)
> For I will turn their mourning into gladness; I will give them comfort and joy instead of sorrow. (Jeremiah 31:13, NIV)
> I bring you good news of great joy that will be for all the people. (Luke 2:10, NIV)

Blessed are you who weep now, for you will laugh. (Luke 6:21, NIV)
Ask and you will receive, and your joy will be complete. (John 16:24, NIV)
[God] will wipe every tear from their eyes. (Revelation 21:4, NIV)
Let there be laughter!

---

[1] Alan Jones, *Sacrifice and Delight* (San Francisco: Harper, 1992), 151.

[2] Ibid.

[3] James Cone, *Martin & Malcolm & America: A Dream or a Nightmare?* (Maryknoll, N.Y.: Orbis Books, 1993), 309.

What's Your Pace Quotient?

The following quiz may help you determine whether or not you need to slow down.

1. You are behind a driver who has not noticed that the light has turned green. How do you respond?

___ (a) Give the person a moment to notice the light has changed

___ (b) Immediately blow your horn

___ (c) Lean on your horn and express your irritation verbally

2. You are in a slow-moving grocery line with time to spare. What are you most likely to do?

___ (a) Engage in conversation with someone

___ (b) Look repeatedly at the person at the register to see how fast things are going

___ (c) Become irritated

3. In conversing with others, how often do you interrupt them in mid-sentence?

___ (a) Not very often

___ (b) Some of the time

___ (c) Very often

4. How much time during the day do you devote to prayer, pondering, meditation, and/or just taking it easy?

___ (a) At least an hour

___ (b) At least 30 minutes

___ (c) Less than 30 minutes

5. Someone/thing has interrupted your planned activity. Select the word that best describes your gut feeling.

___ (a) Interested

___ (b) Disturbed

___ (c) Aggravated

6. Which word best characterizes your mood at the beginning of an average day?

___ (a) Excited

___ (b) Burdened

___ (c) Depressed

7. Which word best describes your emotional state at the end of an average day?

___ (a) Contented

___ (b) Fatigued

___ (c) Stressed

8. When you see a rainbow, how long does it hold your attention?

___ (a) Many minutes

___ (b) Several seconds

___ (c) Just a second

9. When was the last time you paid serious attention to a child?

___ (a) Today

___ (b) Within the past few days

___ (c) I can't remember

10. How often do you feel joy in your work?

___ (a) Frequently

___ (b) Often enough

___ (c) Are you kidding?

11. How often do you hurry one activity to get to the next activity?
___ (a) Not often
___ (b) Regularly
___ (c) All the time

12. How often do you move fast when there is no reason to do so?
___ (a) Never
___ (b) Sometimes
___ (c) I confess: I have rushed through this test!

If you answered (a) for the majority of the questions, chances are you are living at a savoring pace.

If you answered (b) most of the time, paying attention to your pace will be helpful.

If you answered (c) most of the time, paying attention to your pace should become a major priority.

Other Resources Available from the Author

PACE YOURSELF!

Rest in the Storm has introduced you to the life-renewing practice of a "savoring pace": listening more carefully, seeing more clearly, and thinking more deeply.

Savoring Pace Life-Lines are available in a package of fifty cards featuring inspirational thoughts created by Dr. Kirk Jones to help you establish your own savoring pace.

To order your own pack ($7.00 per deck) and perhaps purchase several packs as gifts for others, call Judson Press at 800-458-3766, or order online at www.judsonpress.com.

Also, why not take a moment each week to view Dr. Jones' **Weekly Savoring Pace Life-Line** online at his website, **www.savoringpace.com**?

Keep the Pace and the Pace Will Keep You!

Practical Life-Changing Learning Opportunities

In addition to being available to speak to groups about the relationship between self-care and vocation, Kirk Jones has developed three learning opportunities for clergy and other groups whose work focuses heavily on the needs of others.

Back of the Boat Seminar for Clergy

A three-hour lecture/discussion in which pastors learn how to give themselves permission to experience regular and sufficient periods of recreation and rest. In addition to exploring biblical and theological foundations for self-care, ministers will receive practical guidance on developing a personalized Back of the Boat Schedule and effectively preserving a commitment to self-care amidst the heavy demands of church life.

Back of the Boat Retreat for Clergy

Designed as a beginning-of-the-week respite from the work of ministry, this small-group learning opportunity begins with a supper presentation on Monday evening, continues with presentations and small-group discussions on Tuesday, and concludes with a Wednesday morning closing session and worship experience. More than being an expansion of the Back of the Boat Seminar, the Retreat offers the added benefit of communal sharing and engagement over an extended period of time. This is an ideal opportunity for church and denominational staff who seek to live out self-care as part of their ongoing commitment to professional collegiality. (Limited to 10 Participants)

Savoring Pace Seminar for Caregivers

A 3-hour learning opportunity during which persons from varying high-stress professions are taught how to enhance their daily labor through creating a more peaceful work pace. Special attention will be devoted to teaching persons how to find the balance between satisfying self-care needs and meeting realistic vocational expectations.

For more information on any of the above opportunities or developing your own specialized group learning program, contact Dr. Kirk Jones at 781-961-1816, or e-mail him at kjones58@aol.com.